Witchcraft

A HANDBOOK OF
MAGIC, SPELLS,
AND POTIONS

COMPILED BY ANASTASIA GREYWOLF
ILLUSTRATIONS BY MELISSA WEST

WELLFLEET
PRESS

© 2016 Quarto Publishing Group USA Inc.

First published in 2016 by Wellfleet Press,
an imprint of The Quarto Group
142 West 36th Street, 4th Floor
New York, NY 10018, USA
T (212) 779-4972 F (212) 779-6058
www.QuartoKnows.com

Wellfleet Press titles are also available at discount for retail, wholesale, promotional, and bulk purchase. For details, contact the Special Sales Manager by email at specialsales@quarto.com or by mail at The Quarto Group, Attn: Special Sales Manager, 100 Cummings Center Suite 265D, Beverly, MA 01915 USA.

22

ISBN: 978-1-57715-124-1

A Green Tiger Book
Cover and Interior Design: Susan Livingston
Illustrations © Melissa West
www.greentigerbooks.com

Printed in China TT092020

For entertainment purposes only. Do not attempt any spell, recipe, procedure, or prescription in this book. The author, publisher, packager, manufacturer, distributor, and their collective agents waive all liability for the reader's use or application of any of the text herein.

I conjure thee, O Book, to be useful and profitable unto all who shall have recourse to thee for the success of their affairs. I conjure thee anew, to be serviceable unto all those who shall read thee.

†††

I conjure and command you, O Spirits, all and so many as ye aye, to accept this Book with good grace, so that whensoever we may read it, the same being approved and recognized as in proper form and valid, you shall appear immediately when the conjuration is made, to execute without dallying all that is written and enumerated in its proper place in the said Book. You shall obey, serve, instruct, impart, and perform all in your power for the benefit of those who command you, and the whole without illusion.

†††

CONTENTS

INTRODUCTION

How to Use Witchcraft

Welcome to the world of witchery! The powerful words inside this tome will allow you to effect great change through potions, spells, charms, magic rituals, and incantations. Use them to keep yourself safe, counteract evil, heal disease, find true love, charm animals, obtain great fortune, call upon a storm, speak to the dead, and much more, all through the power of witchcraft and magic.

Time-honored knowledge about the powerful forces that guide our planet comes from all corners of it, so this grimoire combines guidance from many different cultures and religions. Not only does this facilitate you going beyond the realms of traditional American (or even European) witchery, it allows you to consult the spellbooks of the cultures best equipped to administer magic in that area. For instance, while any practitioner of witchcraft would agree that there's no better revenge spell than one from an Italian witches' coven, spells about nature and animals are better handled by a soothing Native American shaman's chant. And while just about every culture has a spell or potion to cure a cough, if you're trying to cure drunkenness, it's best to consult the ancient Gaelic mystics before any others (they recommend procuring an egg from an owl or stork for the drinker's cup).

†††

In the succeeding pages, no differentiation is made between the magic known as *black* and *white*, because what might be considered evil or revengeful in one circumstance might be benevolent in another, especially when viewed through the lens of partisan experience. (However, spells have been separated roughly by purpose into the chapters you find herein.)

Witchcraft means many different things to many different people. But on the whole, it is the study of how to harness energies as well as unleash the power within. With the right tools and a little practice, the words in this tome will allow you to channel aspects of the spiritual world that are beyond the common man or woman to even understand! If you are new to the world of witchcraft, begin with the rest of this introduction, which will instruct you on the proper instruments to practice your craft, as well as how to form a circle with other members of your coven to increase your magical reach.

✝✝✝

For those non-believers who may have found their way to these pages: Before the advent of modern science and medicine, many of the potions and spells in this very book were originally published alongside such practical information as how to prevent an ear infection with alcohol, know what the weather will be based on the wind and clouds, or keep insects away from livestock with vinegar. At the time, all of it was magic. Now, we know that alcohol kills the bacteria that cause ear infections, we can reliably predict the weather within a few degrees (usually), and the acetic acid in vinegar is one of the major components of commercial pesticides. Is it so strange to believe that the accompanying remedies to grow hair, keep fire away, or even regain a lost love might also be based on provable science—but we just haven't discovered it yet?

In this age, what are our remedies for questions that have no answers? Even if you don't believe it is possible to curse an enemy using a mirror, are you not curious as to what a magician would recite at the moment of danger? If a witch has found a mystical avenue to commune with animals, is there not a part of you that wants to know what she does to harness this power?

††††

This belief is the crux of the effectiveness of witchcraft and magic in general. Your power can only match your convictions. As Charles Godfrey Leland, a pioneering researcher into the art of witchcraft, divulged about revenge spells:

> The success of such charms depends chiefly on the seriousness or earnestness with which they are pronounced. When the witch utters them

for herself or for another, she does it with an air
of terrible vindictiveness, such as would cause
anyone to shudder.

Because of this, it's best to try to memorize any words
herein before reciting them, so that they can be said with
the upmost credence. Likewise, anyone who is in your
presence while reciting the spell must also believe in the
efficacy of the pronounced words. Stay calm and if the
desired results are not immediately produced; do not let
emotions overwhelm or discourage you.

✝✝✝

Now, fellow witches and warlocks (whether novice or of
the highest order), go forth and discover what witchcraft
has to offer the world! Use your new magical knowledge
judiciously and without malice. Find those who are like-
minded, and include them in your spiritual practice. And,
if you're so inclined, keep an eye on mystical midnight
moonbeams if you want to catch a glimpse of the magical
doings of my crafty conspirators, the moonbeam coven.

—*Anastasia Greywolf*

Making a Circle

It is most convenient to mark a witch's circle with chalk, paint, or otherwise, to show where it is, but any marks may be utilized; even furniture may be placed to indicate the bounds. You should draw the circle before every ceremony. The circle is usually nine feet in diameter, unless made for some very special purpose. There are two outer circles, each six inches apart, so the third circle has a diameter of eleven feet.

Having chosen a place proper, take an enchanted wand or knife, if thou can obtain one, and stick it into the center. Then take a cord or rope and loop a length of four and one half feet over the instrument (either wand or knife), and so trace out the circumference of the circle. But ever leave open a door toward the North. Make in all three circles, one within the other, and write names of power between these.

When drawing the circles, touch water to your instrument and recite:

> I exorcise thee, O creature of Water, that
> thou cast out from thee all the impurities and
> uncleannesses of the Spirits of the World of
> Phantasm, so they may harm me not, in the
> names of Aradia and Cernunnos.

Touching salt to your instrument, say:

> The Blessings of Aradia and Cernunnos be
> upon this creature of Salt, and let all malignity
> and hindrance be cast forth hencefrom, and
> let all good enter herein, for without thee man
> cannot live, wherefore I bless thee and invoke
> thee, that thou mayest aid me.

Then put the salt into the water. Sprinkle it over the circles. Light candles within the circles and recite:

> I exorcise thee, O creature of Fire, that every
> kind of Phantasm may retire from thee, and be
> unable to harm or deceive in any way, in the
> names of Aradia and Cernunnos.

Circumambulate the circles three times or more before drawing a pentagram (the first stroke of which should be from the top down to the left) with your instrument and commencing work.

Instruments of Witchcraft

THE MAGIC WAND

To make a magic wand, go in search of a rod of wild hazel which has never borne fruit; its length should be nineteen and a half inches. When you have met with a wand of the required form, touch it not otherwise than with your eyes; let it stay till the next morning, when must you cut it absolutely at the moment when the sun rises; strip it of its leaves and lesser branches, if any there be, using an enchanted knife if possible. While cutting, pronounce the following words:

> I beseech Thee, O Grand Adonay, Eloim,
> Ariel, Jehovam, to be propitious unto me, and
> to endow this Wand which I am cutting with
> the power and virtue of the rods of Jacob, of
> Moses, and of the mighty Joshua! I also beseech Thee, O Grand Adonay, Eloim, Ariel,
> Jehovam, to infuse into this Rod the whole
> strength of Samson, the righteous wrath of
> Emanuel, and the thunders of mighty Zariat-natmik, who will avenge the names of men on
> the day of judgment! Amen.

Having pronounced these sublime and terrific words, and still keeping your eyes turned toward the region of the rising sun, you may finish cutting your rod. Before you use the rod, carve a cross where it is held, and inscribe on four different sides of its shaft:

Adonay, Eloim, Ariel, Jehovam.

And thus, it will be prepared for sacred and wonderful works.

SMUDGE STICK

A smudge stick is a bundle of herbs that has been dried and affixed to a stick or staff. It is then set aflame and

used to heighten the efficacy of spells and chants. It may also be used to fumigate objects in order to clear their pasts and prepare them for magical use.

BOLINE KNIFE

A boline knife is a white-handled knife used to describe the circle and inscribe candles and other magical articles. The boline must be forged on the day and in the hour of Jupiter, using a small piece of unused steel. Set it thrice in the fire and extinguish it in the blood of a mole mixed with the juice of the pimpernel. Let this be done when the Moon is in her full light and course. On the same day and in the hour of Jupiter, fit a horn handle to the steel, shaping it with a new sword forged thrice as above in the fire. When made and perfected (or purchased from one who has done so), recite over it this:

> I conjure thee, O form of this instrument, by the authority of God the Father Almighty, by the virtue of Heaven and the stars, by the virtue of the Angels, by that of the elements, by that of stones and herbs, and in like manner by the virtue of snowstorms, thunder, and winds, that thou receive all power unto the performance of those things in the perfection of which we are concerned, the whole without trickery, falsehood, or deception, by the command of God, Creator of the ages and Emperor of the Angels. Amen.

Place it in a new wrapper of red silk until ready for use.

PEN AND INK

The instruments one uses to complete spells are of the utmost importance. If possible, craft a quill thusly: Pluck the third feather from the right wing of a male goose, and say, extracting it:

> Arbarchay, Araton, Samatoy, Scaver, Adonay!
> Expel all evil from this feather, so that it may
> possess full power to write whatsoever I will.

Then shape it with a boline knife. Lastly, take a new ink-horn, made on the day and in the hour of Venus, and write about it these names with the exorcised lancet of the Art:

> Jod, He, Vau, He, Mitatron, Jae, Jae, Jae,
> Cados, Eloyn, Zevao.

Then dip the pen therein, pronouncing the following words:

> I exorcise thee, creature of the feather kind,
> by Etereton, by Samatoy, and by the name
> Adonay. Do thou aid me in all my works.

DOLL BABY (VOODOO DOLL)

To make a doll baby (voodoo doll), fill a small cloth sack with herbs and flora as well as any personal objects from its original likeness and use twine to fashion a head, arms, and legs. Once the doll baby is created, baptize it in whiskey, saying:

> By the gods good and bad, I baptize thee,
> [Name of victim].

From this point forth, use the name of the doll baby every time you address it. Every action you perform on it will be reflected in your target. To bind your enemy, tie the doll's hands; to bind your enemy to another person, tie it to another doll; for love spells, pierce its heart; for menace, pierce its genitals; pin the doll down entirely to keep its likeness away from you entirely.

WISH BOX

A wish box is a magical object that helps wishes come true. You can obtain your wish box from a sorcerer, carve one out of wood, or even fold one out of paper.

Inscribe wishes, goals, and desires on separate sheets of paper. Fold the paper as many times as possible and place in the box. Meditate.

SILKEN CLOTH

When all the instruments have been completed, they must be gathered into a costly cloth of silk, whereby they may be preserved clean and pure and may thus be more efficacious. As long as it be not black or brown, the color is indifferent, but the following characters must be written upon it in pigeon's blood with a male goose-quill:

> Adonay, Ammastius, Anareton, Cosbos, Eloym.

Place all magical instruments in this silken cloth and repeat:

> So shall I use thee at will and shall learn their effect.

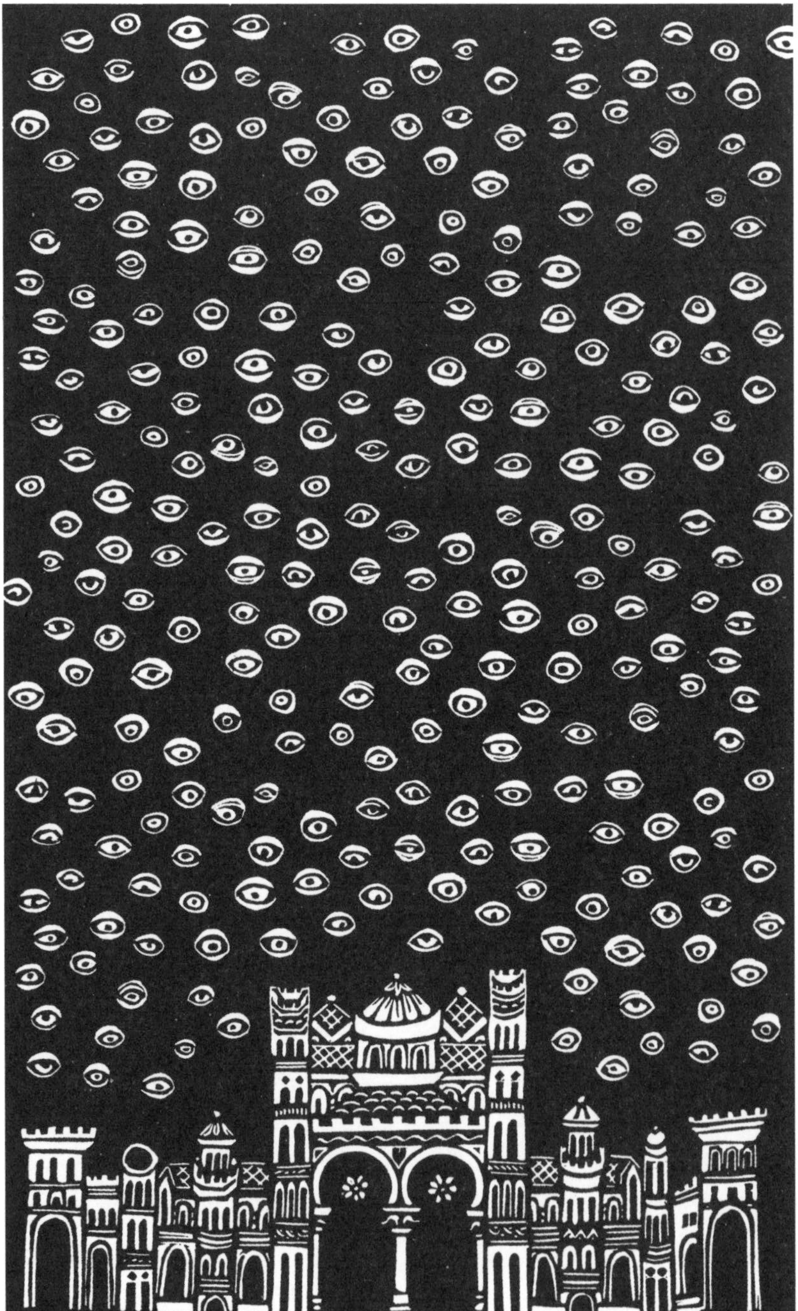

SAFEKEEPING

FOR SAFEKEEPING
AMERICAN MAGICIAN'S INCANTATION

For safekeeping, recite every morning:

> Grant me, oh Lord, a good and pleasant hour,
> that all sick people may recover, and all dis-
> tressed in body or mind, repose or grace may
> find, and guardian angel may over them hover;
> and all those captive and in bondage fettered,
> may have their conditions and troubles bet-
> tered; for all good travelers on horse or foot, we
> wish a safe journey, joyful and good, and good
> women in labor and toil, a safe delivery and joy.

TO PROTECT ONESELF AT
THE MOMENT OF DANGER
AMERICAN MAGICIAN'S SPELL

Repeat reverently, and with sincere faith, the following
words, and you shall be protected in the hour of danger:

> He shall deliver thee in six troubles, yea in
> seven there shall no evil touch thee.

> In famine he shall redeem thee from death, and
> in war from the power of the sword.

> And thou shall know that thy tabernacle shall
> be peace, and thy habitation shall not err.

TO PREVENT INJURIES
POW-WOW CHARM

Whoever carries the right eye of a wolf fastened inside his right sleeve remains free from all injuries.

FOR PROTECTION AGAINST TREACHEROUS DESIGNS
ANCIENT HINDU INCANTATION

For protection against the treacherous designs of others, recite:

> The great guardian among these gods sees as if from anear. He that thinketh he is moving stealthily—all this the gods know.
>
> If a man stands, walks, or sneaks about, if he goes slinking away, if he goes into his hiding-place; if two persons sit together and scheme; King Varuna is there as a third, and knows it.
>
> Both this earth belongs to King Varuna, and also yonder broad sky whose boundaries are far away. Moreover these two oceans are the

loins of Varuna; yea, he is hidden in this drop of water.

He that should flee beyond the heavens, far away, would not be free from King Varuna. His spies come hither from heaven, with a thousand eyes do they watch over the Earth.

King Varuna sees through all that is between heaven and the earth, and all that is beyond. He has counted the winkings of men's eyes. As a winning gamester puts down his dice, thus does he establish these laws.

May all thy fateful toils which, seven by seven, threefold, lie spread out, ensnare him that speaks falsehood: him that speaks the truth; they shall let go!

With a hundred snares, O Varuna, surround him, let the liar not go free from thee, O thou that observest men! The rogue shall sit, his belly hanging loose, like a cask without hoops, bursting all about!

With the snare of Varuna which is fastened lengthwise, and that which is fastened broad-wise, with the indigenous and the foreign, with the divine and the human,

With all these snares do I fetter thee, O
[Name], descended from [Name], the son
of the woman [Name]: all these do I design
for thee.

FOR SAFEKEEPING AGAINST THE WICKED
GAELIC SPELL

To keep thyself safe against the wicked, recite:

> The wicked who would do me harm
> May he take the throat disease
> Globularly, spirally, circularly,
> Fluxy, pellety, horny-grim.
>
> Be it harder than the stone,
> Be it blacker than the coal,
> Be it swifter than the duck,
> Be it heavier than the lead.
>
> Be it fiercer, fiercer, sharper, harsher, more
>   malignant,
> Than the hard, wound-quivering holly,
> Be it sourer than the sained, lustrous,
>   bitter salt salt,
> Seven seven times.

Oscillating thither,
Undulating hither,
Staggering downwards,
Floundering upwards,
Driveling outwards,
Sniveling inwards,
Oft hurrying out,
Seldom coming in.

A wisp the portion of each hand,
A foot in the base of each pillar,
A leg the prop of each jamb,
A flux driving and dragging him.

A dysentery of blood from the heart, from
    form, from bones,
From the liver, from the lobe, from the lungs,
And a searching of veins, of throat, and of
    kidneys,
To my condemners and traducers.

In the name of the God of might,
Who warded from me every evil,
And who shielded me in strength,
From the net of my breakers
And destroyers.

TO DETER MALICIOUS PERSONS
POW-WOW SPELL

To prevent wicked or malicious persons from doing you an injury, against whom this spell has great power, recite:

> *Dullix, ix, ux.* Yea, you can't come over Pontio;
> Pontio is above Pilato.

TO SECURE MAN AND BEAST AGAINST ALL MISFORTUNES
GYPSY INCANTATION

Three Fridays in succession, in the morning, this should be repeated three times over house and all the estates, and thereby a golden ring shall be manufactured, by which not only house and home but also man and beast will be secured against all misfortunes and pestilential epidemics and diseases, and are secured against the arts and wiles of the powers of the devil:

> May God, the Father, make a golden ring
> around this house, around this stable, around
> all men and beasts that belongeth thereto and
> goeth in and out of it; also around my fields
> and forests, yea, this very ring encircles our
> beloved Mary with her dear infant, Jesus Christ
> they protect, watch over, maintain, shelter,
> cover and defend all mankind, both male and

female, small and large, young and old, as
likewise, all cattle, oxen, steers, cows and calves,
horses and foals, sheep, goats, beef-cattle and
swine, geese, ducks, chickens, pigeons, large
and small, whatever is contained in this house
and these stables and all that cometh in and
goeth out; for all misfortunes, evil, colic, wild-
fire, losses, epidemics, and other diseases; for all
bad and heated blood; for all bad and malicious enemies and storms; for all evil hours, day
and night; for all magic power of witchcraft,
and the designs and powers of the devil and his
infernal hosts, to be visible or invisible, or for all
wicked people who contemplate to rob me, that
they may not be able to carry or spoil aught,
anything that these people and animals, young
and old, large and small, nothing excepted,
whatsoever belongeth to these premises and
their surroundings, and goeth out and cometh
in, from whence and hence that no loss may occur, nor any evil be done at home or abroad, in
the field or in the woods, in the meadows and
on the plains, in grass, wood, or heath, whether
it works or rests, sits, lays, runs, or stands, they
shall all now for all time to come be included
in this ring, and be secure and protected from
bullet and sword, by the very holy blood-drops
of the dear beloved infant, Jesus Christ, which

he hath suffered and shed for us by his circumcision and upon the cross and thereby vouchsafed and sealed his love everlasting, for such, they, the magicians, will find no herb which may open, break or move or pervert, because our dear Lord Jesus Christ protects and defendeth such with his ever holy hands, and his supremely sacred five wounds, at all times, by day and by night, and at all hours, forever and ever eternally. In the name of God the Father, the Son, and the Holy Spirit.

TO OBSTRUCT FIRE'S FLAMES
POW-WOW SPELL

In order to obstruct fire's flames, recite:

The bitter sorrows and the death of our dear Lord Jesus Christ shall prevail. Fire and wind and great heat and all that is within the power of these elements, I command thee, through the Lord Jesus Christ, who has spoken to the winds and the waters, and they obeyed him. By these powerful words spoken by Jesus, I command, threaten, and inform thee, fire, flame, and heat, and your powers as elements, to flee forthwith. The holy, rosy blood of our dear Lord Jesus Christ may rule it. Thou, fire, and wind, and great beat, I command thee, as the Lord did, by his holy angels, command the great heat in the fiery oven to leave those three holy men, Shadrach and his companions, Meshach and Abednego, untouched, which was done accordingly. Thus thou shall abate, thou fire, flame, and great heat, the Almighty God having spoken in creating the four elements, together with heaven and earth: Fiat! Fiat! Fiat! That is: It shall be in the name of God the Father, the Son, and the Holy Ghost. Amen.

TO PREVENT YOUR HOME FROM CATCHING AFLAME
GYPSY POTION

To enchant a house so that it is protected from all dangers of fire, although the flames may surround it, take in the evening or in the morning a black hen from its nest, cut its throat, and throw it upon the ground. Cut the stomach of the hen from out of the body, but nothing else, and be careful to leave everything else inside. After this proceeding obtain a piece of gold quartz. The piece must be large as a saucer. These two articles, wrap them up together. Take an egg laid on Maundy Thursday. Wrap the three pieces thus obtained in beeswax and put all in an octagonal pot of clay. Cover the same tightly and bury it under the house doorsill.

 ## TO AVERT PERIL WHEN FACED WITH FIRE OR WATER
AMERICAN MAGICIAN'S SPELL

Repeat reverently, and with sincere faith, the following words, and you shall be protected in the hour of danger:

> When thou passest through the waters, I will be with thee, and through the rivers, they shall not overflow thee; when thou walkest through the fire, thou shall not be burnt, neither shall the flame kindle upon thee.

TO KEEP YOUR HOME FROM HARM
ANCIENT HINDU INCANTATION

To keep your home from harm, at its building, recite:

> Right here do I erect a firm house: may it stand
> upon a good foundation, dripping with ghee!
> Thee may we inhabit, O house, with heroes all,
> with strong heroes, with uninjured heroes!

> Right here, do thou, O house, stand firmly, full
> of horses, full of cattle, full of abundance! Full
> of sap, full of ghee, full of milk, elevate thyself
> unto great happiness!

> A supporter art thou, O house, with broad roof,
> containing purified grain! To thee may the calf
> come, to thee the child, to thee the milk-cows,
> when they return in the evening!

> May Savitar, Vâyu, Indra, Brihaspati cunningly
> erect this house! Alay and Alaruts, sprinkle it
> with moisture and with ghee; may King Bhaga
> let our ploughing take root!

O mistress of dwelling, as a sheltering and kindly goddess thou wast erected by the gods in the bealrinina; clothed in grass, be thou kindly disposed; give us, moreover, wealth along with heroes!

Do thou, O cross-beam, according to regulation ascend the post, do thou, mightily ruling, hold off the enemies! May they that approach thee reverently, O house, not suffer injury, may we with all our heroes live a hundred autumns!

Hither to this house hath come the tender child, hither the calf along with the other domestic animals; hither the vessel full of liquor, together with bowls of sour milk!

Carry forth, O woman, this full jar, a stream of ghee mixed with ambrosia! Do thou these drinkers supply with ambrosia; the sacrifice and the gifts to the Brahmans shall it protect!

These waters, free from disease, destructive of disease, do I carry forth. The chambers do I enter in upon together with the immortal fire.

FOR SAFEKEEPING THROUGH A TOWN
GYPSY CHARM

If your whipstick's made of rowan,
You can ride your nag through any town.

FOR SAFEKEEPING WHILST TRAVELING
GYPSY SPELL

To secure oneself against wicked people whilst travel-
ing, and if in being danger of being attacked, speak three
times:

> Two wicked eyes have overshadowed me, but
> three other eyes are overshadowing me too,
> the one of God the Father, the other of God
> the Son, the third of God the Holy Spirit; they
> watch my blood and flesh, my marrow and
> bone, and all other large and small limbs; they
> shall be protected in the name of God.

TO PROTECT A BABY YET TO BE BORN
AMERICAN WITCH'S CHARM

To protect an unborn child, encase a branch of myrtle in
a soft cloth. Place candles in a pentagram shape around
the cloth. Recite five times:

> By Eileithyia, by Hera, learn your mother's
> words from her own mouth, baby, come forth
> so that we may hear thy cry.

HEALING

Spells

AND POTIONS

TO CURE SICKNESS
POW-WOW RITUAL

This remedy is to be applied when anyone is sick, and has effected many a cure where doctors could not help. Let the sick person, without having conversed with anyone, put water in a bottle before sunrise, close it tightly, and put it immediately in some box or chest. Lock it and stop up the keyhole (the key must be carried in one of the pockets for three days, as nobody dare have it except the person who puts the bottle with water in the chest or box). The sickness will improve.

TO BANISH A HEADACHE
GYPSY SPELL

To banish a headache, rub the head of the afflicted with vinegar and hot water while reciting:

> Oh, pain in my head,
> The father of all evil,
> Look upon thee now!
> Thou hast greatly pained me,
> Thou tormentest my head,
> Remain not in me!

Go thou, go thou, go home,
Whence thou, Evil One, didst suck,
Thither, thither hasten!
Who treads upon my shadow,
To him be the pain!

TO IMPROVE MEMORY
AMERICAN MAGICIAN'S POTION

When a person has a weak head and is often absent-minded, take hold of an ant's hill, then put it in a bag, and boil the same for six hours in a kettle of water. Draw this water upon bottles and distill it in the sun. With such water wash the weak and dull head. If the disease is very bad, bathe the patient in this water.

TO WARD OFF INSOMNIA
GYPSY CHARM

To facilitate healthy sleep, procure two rabbit ears. Place them under the pillow of the person who cannot sleep, without his knowledge.

FOR EASING PAIN IN THE EYES
GYPSY SPELL

Pain in the eyes is cured with a wash made of spring or well water and saffron. During the application, recite:

> Oh, pain from the eyes
> Go into the water,
> Go out of the water
> Into the saffron,
> Go out of the saffron
> Into the earth.
> To the Earth-Spirit.
> There's thy home.
> There go and eat.

TO CAST OFF STYES
ANCIENT MACEDONIAN CHARM

A small wart, which sometimes appears on the lower eyelid and which, from its shape, is known as a little grain of barley, is cured if someone bearing a rare name barks at it like a dog.

TO IMPROVE HEARING
GYPSY CHARM

Take the oil with which the bells of churches are greased, and smear it behind the afflicted ears, and relief will not fail to come at once for those who could not formerly hear the bells.

TO REPEL COUGH
ANCIENT HINDU INCANTATION

As a remedy against cough, recite:

> As the soul with the soul's desires swiftly to a distance flies, thus do thou, O cough, fly forth along the soul's course of flight!

> As a well-sharpened arrow swiftly to a distance flies, thus do thou, O cough, fly forth along the expanse of the earth!

> As the rays of the sun swiftly to a distance fly, thus do thou, O cough, fly forth along the flood of the sea!

TO VANQUISH TOOTHACHE
GYPSY CHARM

To vanquish a person's toothache, write down, with a newly made goose-quill (having been careful that nothing was wasted from the quill but what belongs to shape the pen) and ink, on the outside of the cheek where the pain is situated, the following signs:

MOT, TOT, FOT.

After this is done, light a candle, and proceed therewith under the chimney. Burn the pen by the light under the hearth, until not a vestige thereof remains. All this must be done noiselessly, while the person who suffers the pain must at once put her head in a bandage, retire to bed, and remain quiet, and by no means speak a word to anybody for twenty-four hours.

TO CEASE EXCESSIVE DISCHARGES
ANCIENT HINDU INCANTATION

To cease excessive discharges from the body, recite:

> We know the father of the arrow, Parganya,
> who furnishes bountiful fluid, and well do
> we know his mother, Prithivi (Earth), the
> multiform!

> O bowstring, turn aside from us, turn my body
> into stone! Do thou firmly hold very far away
> the hostile powers and the haters!

> When the bowstring, embracing the wood of
> the bow, greets with a whiz the arrow, do thou,
> O Indra, ward off from us the piercing missile!

> As the point of the arrow stands in the way of
> heaven and the earth, thus may the muñga-
> grass unfailingly stand in the way of sickness
> and excessive discharge!

TO REMEDY BURNS
POW-WOW SPELL

To remedy burns, recite:

> Clear out, brand, but never in; be thou cold or
> hot, thou must cease to burn. May God guard
> thy blood and thy flesh, thy marrow and thy
> bones, and every artery, great or small. They all
> shall be guarded and protected in the name of
> God against inflammation and mortification, in
> the name of God the Father, the Son, and the
> Holy Ghost. Amen.

TO EASE BURNS
GYPSY SPELL

To ease the pain of a burn, speak three times:

> Away burns, undo the band; if cold or warm,
> cease the hand. God save thee, [Name]; thy
> flesh, thy blood, thy marrow, thy bone, and all
> thy veins. They all shall be saved, for warm and
> cold brands reign.

TO BANISH PIMPLES
ANCIENT MACEDONIAN CHARM

If thou wish to banish marks of the face, repair before sunrise to a lonely spot where there is a quince-tree, and, standing naked beneath its bough, pronounce three times the following (whether thou art man or woman):

> I want a man and want him at once!

Then pick up your clothes and walk off forty paces, without looking back. Having reached that point, stop and dress.

This must be done three days in succession.

TO DRIVE AWAY WARTS
GYPSY SPELL

Speak over warts this:

> Vanish in flaming ether, salamander! Flow together, step forward, and finish thus, in the name of God the Father, God the Son, and God the Holy Spirit.

This must be repeated three times, and each time, while pronouncing the three holiest names, blow over the warts, and in a very few weeks they will vanish, so that none will know whence they have gone to.

 ## TO GET RID OF SWOLLEN GLANDS
ANCIENT MACEDONIAN CHARM

To rid oneself of swollen glands, write any passage from a religious work like the Bible on your cheek or neck. Or, wet torn-out pages and place them on the ailment.

FOR DRUNKENNESS
GAELIC CHARM

The eggs of an owl or a stork put into the cup of a drunkard will cause a loathing of liquor and cure the habit of drinking.

TO TREAT ONE WHO IS BITTEN BY A SNAKE
CHEROKEE SHAMAN'S CHARM

To treat one who has been bitten by a snake, rub tobacco juice on the bite for some time, or if there be no tobacco just rub on saliva once. In rubbing it on, one must go around four times. Go around toward the left and blow four times in a circle. (This is because in lying down, the snake always coils to the right.) Pronounce:

> Listen! Ha! It is only a common frog that has
> passed by and put the poison in you.
> Listen! Ha! It is only an Us'gï that passed by.
> Listen! Ha! It is only an Us'gï that passed by.
> Listen! Ha! It is only a common frog that has
> passed by and put the poison in you.
> Listen! Ha! It is only an Us'gï which has passed
> by and put the poison in you.

TO COUNTERACT POISON
ANCIENT HINDU INCANTATION

If thou wishest to counteract poison, recite:

> The Brâhmana was the first to be born, with ten heads and ten mouths. He was the first to drink the soma; that did render poison powerless.

> As great as heaven and earth are in extent, as far as the seven streams did spread, so far from here have I proclaimed forth this charm that destroys poison.

> The eagle Garutmant did, O poison, first devour thee. Thou didst not bewilder him, didst not injure him, yea, thou didst turn into food for him.

> The five-fingered hand that did hurl upon thee the arrow, even from the curved bow—from the point of the arrow have I charmed away the poison.

> From the point have I charmed away the poison, from the substance that has been smeared upon it, and from its plume. From its barbed horn, and its neck, I have charmed away the poison.

Powerless, O arrow, is thy point, and powerless is thy poison. Moreover of powerless wood is thy powerless bow, O powerless arrow!

They that ground the poison, they that daubed it on, they that hurled it, and they that let it go, all these have been rendered impotent. The mountain that grows poisonous plants has been rendered impotent.

Impotent are they who dig thee, impotent art thou, O plant! Impotent is that mountain height whence this poison has sprung.

TO EASE RHEUMATISM
CHEROKEE SHAMAN'S RITUAL

To ease rheumatism, place hands on the body of the afflicted and recite:

Yû! O Red Woman, you have caused it. You have put the intruder under him. Ha! now you have come from the Sun Land. You have brought the small red seats, with your feet resting upon them. Ha! now they have swiftly moved away from you. Relief is accomplished. Let it not be for one night alone. Let the relief come at once.

(If treating a man one must say "Red Woman," and if treating a woman one must say "Red Man.")

Remove the hands and blow once, then replace the hands and recite three more times. After the final recitation, blow four times.

Then apply to afflicted areas: the bear's bed fern, the cinnamon fern, the crow's shin, and what is called the beaver's paw. Boil the roots of these plants together and apply in the evening for four consecutive nights.

For seven nights, these are taboo: One must not touch a squirrel, a dog, a cat, the mountain trout, or women. He who is being treated must sit on a seat by himself for four nights, and must not sit on any other seat for these four nights.

TO COMBAT CHEST PAIN
ANCIENT MACEDONIAN SPELL

For pain in the breast, say this:

> Saint Kosmas and Damian, Cyrus and Saint John, Saint Nicholas and Saint Akindynos, who hold the scythes and cut the pain, cut also the pain of the servant of God [Name of afflicted person].

TO CURE FEVER
POW-WOW SPELL

In the early morning, turn your shirt around the left sleeve and say:

> Turn, thou, shirt, and thou, fever, do likewise
> turn [Name of afflicted person]. This, I tell
> thee, for thy repentance sake, in the name of
> God the Father, the Son, and the Holy Ghost.
> Amen.

If you repeat this for three successive mornings the fever will disappear.

TO CURE FEVER IN ONESELF
GYPSY SPELL

To cure fever in oneself, go to a running stream and cast pieces of wood nine times backwards into the running water, repeating as you do so:

> Fever go away from me,
> I give it, water, unto thee
> Unto me thou art not dear,
> Therefore go away from here
> To where they nursed thee,
> Where they shelter thee,
> Where they love thee,
> Mashurdalo—help!

FOR THE FALLING SICKNESS (EPILEPSY)
GAELIC CHARM

To make the falling sickness depart from a person, take a hank of grey yarn, a lock of the patient's hair, and some parings of his nails, and bury them deep in the earth, repeating, as if a burial service:

> Let the great sickness lie there forever. By the power of Mary and the soul of Paul, let the great sickness lie buried in the clay, and nevermore rise out of the ground. Amen.

If the patient, on awaking from sleep, calls out the name of the person who uttered these words, his recovery is certain.

If a person crosses over the patient while he is in a fit, or stands between him and the fire, then the sickness will cleave to him and depart from the other who was afflicted.

TO HEAL A SPRAIN
GAELIC SPELL

To heal a sprain, wrap a strand of black wool round the area, and recite in a low voice:

> The Lord rade and the foal slade,
> He lighted and He righted;
> Set joint to joint and bone to bone,
> And sinew unto sinew.
> In the name of God and the Saints,
> Of Mary and her Son,
> Let this man be healed. Amen.

TO EASE NIGHT CRAMPS
GYPSY SPELL

To ease night cramps, recite:

> There is a mighty hill, and on this hill is a golden apple-tree,
>
> Under the golden apple-tree is a golden stool.
>
> On the stool—who sits there?
>
> There sits the Mother of God with Saint Maria; with the boxes in her right hand, with the cup in her left.

She looks up and sees naught, she looks down and sees my Lord and Lady Disease, Lords and Ladies Cramp, Lord and Lady Vampire, Lord Werewolf and his wives.

They are going to [Name], to drink her blood and put in her a foul heart.

The Mother of God, when she sees them, goes down to them, speaks to them, and asks them, "Whither go ye, Lord and Lady Disease, Lords and Ladies Cramp?"

"We go to [Name] to drink her blood, to change her heart to a foul one."

"No, ye shall return; give her her blood back, restore her own heart, and leave her immediately."

Cramps of the night, cramps of the midnight, cramps of the day, cramps wherever they are. From the water, from the wind, go out from the brain, from the light of the face, from the hearing of the ears, from her heart, from her hands and feet, from the soles of her feet.

Go and hide where cocks never crow, where men never go, where no beast roars.

Hide yourself there, stop there, and never show yourself more!

May [Name] remain pure and glad, as she was made by God, and was fated by the Mother of God!

The spell is mine—the cure is God's.

TO PREVENT MISCARRIAGE
ANCIENT ASIATIC SPELL

If a woman is carrying a child, she should recite:

Just as the earth creates, so shall, in a like manner, a child be potently produced! The embryo shall be guarded as if by mountains, and a child shall be born in safekeeping.

FOR WHEN LABOR IS DIFFICULT
GYPSY POTION

If labor, when it comes, is difficult, give the mother another's milk to drink, or a parsnip that must be finely bruised; tie the same over the body, and she will soon be easy and come to rest.

TO MAKE A CHILD "JUMP DOWN" (BE BORN AT ONCE)
CHEROKEE SHAMAN'S SPELL

To make a boy child jump down, cry out:

> Listen! You little man, get up now at once.
> There comes an old woman. The horrible old
> lady is coming, only a little way off. Listen!
> Quick! Get your bed and let us run away. *Yû!*

To make a girl child jump down, cry out:

> Listen! You little woman, get up now at once.
> There comes your grandfather. The horrible
> old fellow is coming, only a little way off.
> Listen! Quick! Get your bed and let us run
> away. *Yû!*

Blow dust of a yellow root on the forehead of the mother while reciting, and the child will be frightened into coming into the world.

Spells
AGAINST ENEMIES

 TO WARD OFF ENEMIES
AMERICAN MAGICIAN'S INCANTATION

Repeat reverently, and with sincere faith, the following words, and you shall be protected in the hour of danger:

> Behold, I will trust, and not be afraid, for stars
> of Heaven, and the constellations thereof, shall
> not give their light; the sun shall be darkened in
> his going forth, and the moon shall not cause
> her light to shine. And behold, at evening tide,
> trouble; and before the morning is not; this in
> the portion of them that spoils us.

TO INJURE A FOE
TUSCAN WITCH'S CHARM

To make a man or woman suffer, take a peppercorn such as is found in the fields, and boil it with the hair of your foe and recite:

> I do not boil the hair alone,
> But all these things together thrown,
> With his heart and soul that he,
> May perish and forever be
> Only in witches' company.

TO MAKE AN ENEMY SUFFER
TUSCAN WITCH'S CHARM

To cause suffering in an enemy, obtain a toad as well as some of the hairs of your victim. Tie them to the left leg of the toad, and put the animal into a covered pot. As it suffers the enemy will suffer; when it dies he will die. But if you wish your enemy only to suffer and not die, remove the hair from the leg of the toad and let it go.

 TO CURSE AN ENEMY USING SALT AND PEPPER
TUSCAN WITCH'S CHARM

To curse an enemy, take salt and pepper and put it into his clothing or in his house, and say:

> I put this pepper on you,
> And this salt thereto,
> That peace and happiness
> You nevermore may know.

TO CURSE AN ENEMY USING A MIRROR
AMERICAN WITCH'S CHARM

Constructing a mirror in the following way can be used to great effect on your enemies: Take a mirror in a wooden frame and put it into a tub of water, so that it will swim on the top with its face directed toward the sky. On the top of the mirror and encircling the glass, lay a wreath, and thus expose it to the influence of the new moon. This evil influence is thrown toward the moon, and radiating again from the moon it may bring evil to those who have to look upon it.

The rays of the moon passing through that ring upon the mirror become poisoned, and poison the mirror; and the mirror throws back ether to the atmosphere, and the moon and mirror poison each other in the same manner as two malicious persons looking at each other, poisoning each other's souls with their eyes.

If a mirror is strongly poisoned in this manner, and the witch takes good care of it, and if she desires to injure someone, she may take a waxen image made in his name, surround it with a cloth spotted with menstrual blood, and throw the reflection of the mirror onto the figure, using at the same time her evil imagination and curses. The man whom the image represents may then have his vitality dried up and his blood poisoned by that evil influence, and he may become diseased and his body covered with boils.

TO DISCERN AN ADVERSARY'S NEFARIOUS DESIGNS
GYPSY CHARM

To discern at a distance of three miles or more what an adversary designs, obtain a plain looking glass, as large as you please, and have it framed on three sides only; upon the left side it should be left open. Such a glass must be held toward the direction where the enemy is existing and you will be able to discern all his markings, maneuverings, his doings and workings.

FOR DEPRIVING ENEMIES OF THEIR STRENGTH
ANCIENT HINDU INCANTATION

To deprive enemies of their strength, recite:

> As the rising sun takes away the luster of the stars, thus do I take away the strength of both the women and the men who hate me.

> As many enemies as ye are, looking out against me, as I come on—of those who hate me do I take away your strength, as the sun takes away the strength of person's sleep as it rises.

❀❀ TO HINDER A RIVAL FROM KILLING ANY GAME

EUROPEAN MAGICIAN'S RITUAL

Perform this rite to hinder a rival from accurately taking aim at or killing any game. Take a stick of green elder, from the two ends of which thou shall clean out the pith inside. In each end place a strip of parchment of hareskin, having written thereon with the blood of a black hen the name of the victim. Having made two of these slips, place one in each end of the stick and close the apertures up with pith. Afterward, on a Friday in the month of February, thou shall fumigate the aforesaid stick with suitable incense thrice in the air, and having taken it thence thou shall bury it in the earth under an elder-tree. Afterward, thou shall expose it in the pathway by which the sportsman will pass, and once he has passed by it, he need not hope to kill any game during that day. If thou shall wish a second time to lay a spell upon him in like manner, thou needest but to expose the stick again in his path; but take care to bury it again in the earth under an elder-tree, so as to be able to take it from thence each time that thou shall have need of it; and to take it up each time as soon as the victim shall have passed.

TO PREVENT OTHERS FROM HITTING A TARGET
GYPSY CHARM

To hinder others in shooting a target, put a splinter of wood which has been hit by a thunderbolt behind it. No person will be able to hit such a target.

TO PREVENT AN ENEMY FROM FIRING A GUN
GYPSY SPELL

To keep a person from firing a gun whilst you are looking into the barrel, pronounce:

Pax, Sax, Sxrax.

TO DETECT A THIEF
POW-WOW CHARM

Collect together laurel leaves and the tooth of a wolf in the sign of the lion (the month of August). If anything has been stolen, put this under your head during the night, and you will surely see the whole figure of the thief.

TO COMPEL A THIEF TO RETURN STOLEN PROPERTY

GYPSY CHARM

It is possible to compel a thief to return stolen property. Obtain a new earthenware pot with a cover, and draw water from the undercurrent of a stream while calling out the three holiest names. Fill the vessel one-third, take the same to your home, and set it upon the fire. Take a piece of bread from the lower crust of a loaf, stick three pins into the bread, and boil in the vessel with a few dew nettles. Then say:

> Thief, male or female, bring my stolen articles back, whether thou art boy or girl; thief, if thou art woman or man, I compel thee, in the name of the Father, Son, and Holy Spirit.

TO PREVENT A PERSON FROM ESCAPING
GYPSY CHARM

Take a needle wherewith the gown of a corpse was sewed, and draw this needle through the hat or shoe of him whom you seek to fasten, and he cannot escape.

TO BANISH YOUR ENEMY
AMERICAN MAGICIAN'S POTION

To banish your enemy, collect dirt from his shoes or clothing. Mix it with cayenne pepper, then grind it with sassafras and coffee grounds, preferably those used to make coffee your enemy drank. Sprinkle the mixture in front of your enemy's door and he will leave your community.

FOR BANISHING SOMEONE WITH FOUR THIEVES' VINEGAR
HOODOO CHARM

To banish someone, mix the potion known as four thieves' vinegar. Combine together apple cider vinegar, rosemary, sage, lavender, wormwood, and camphor. Place the concoction in a jar in a dark corner for two months before opening. Then apply to the doorknob of the person you wish to banish.

TO RID YOUR HOME OF UNWANTED HOUSEGUESTS
AMERICAN MAGICIAN'S CHARM

To get rid of a person who has overstayed his welcome at your home, go to the market and choose an onion that reminds you most of your guest. Inscribe the name of your guest on a piece of parchment five times. Slice the onion in half, then remove the center orb and place the parchment inside. Place the pieces of onion back together and seal with whatever means available.

After your guest has walked out your home's front entrance, roll the onion across its threshold, before anyone else has left or entered. Bury the onion immediately as far away as possible; do not bring it inside your home again.

TO CURSE A FAITHLESS LOVER
GYPSY CHARM

If a maid has a faithless lover, she may curse him in the following manner. Light a candle at midnight and prick it several times with a needle, saying:

> Thrice the candle's broke by me
> Thrice thy heart shall broken be!

If the faithless lover marries another, the deceived maid should mix the broken shell of a crab in his food or drink, or hide one of her hairs in a bird's nest. This will make the new marriage unhappy, and the husband will continually pine for his neglected sweetheart.

TO DEPRIVE A MAN OF HIS VIRILITY
ANCIENT HINDU INCANTATION

If a man is undeserving of his virility, you can deprive him by reciting:

> As the best of the plants thou art reputed, O herb: turn this man for me today into a eunuch that wears his hair dressed!

> Turn him into a eunuch that wears his hair dressed, and into one that wears a hood! Then Indra with a pair of stones shall break his testicles both!

> O eunuch, into a eunuch thee I have turned; O castrate, into a castrate thee I have turned; O weakling, into a weakling thee I have turned! A hood upon his head, and a hair-net do we place.

> The two canals, fashioned by the gods, in which man's power rests, in thy testicles . . . I break them with a club.

> As women break reeds for a mattress with a stone, thus do I break thy member.

FOR KEEPING A ROMANTIC RIVAL AWAY
ANCIENT HINDU INCANTATION

If a woman has designs on a maid's sweetheart, the maid may recite:

> I have taken unto myself her fortune and her glory, as a wreath off a tree. Like a mountain with broad foundation may she sit a long time with her parents!

> This woman shall be subjected to thee as thy wife, O King Yama; till then let her be fixed to the house of her mother, or her brother, or her father!

> This woman shall be the keeper of thy house, O King Yama! May she long sit with her relatives, until her hair drops from her head!

> With the incantation of Asita, of Kasyapa, and of Gaya do I cover up thy fortune, as women cover what lies within a chest.

TO SEPARATE TWO LOVERS
CHEROKEE SHAMAN'S SPELL

If a jealous rival so desires, speak this to separate two lovers:

> *Yû!* On high you repose, O Blue Hawk, there at the far distant lake. The blue tobacco has come to be your recompense. Now you have arisen at once and come down. You have alighted midway between them where they two are standing. You have spoiled their souls immediately. They have at once become separated.

TO CAUSE HATRED BETWEEN LOVERS
GAELIC CHARM

To cause hatred between lovers, take a handful of clay from a newly made grave and shake it between them, saying:

> Hate ye one another! May ye be as hateful to each other as sin to Christ, as bread eaten without blessing is to God.

TO CURSE A BRIDE'S MARRIAGE
TUSCAN WITCH'S CHARM

If you desire that a woman shall never find happiness in marriage, take on her wedding-day an orange flower, and put into it a little salt, pepper, and cumin, with discordia, and attach this to the bride's back, saying:

> Be thou accursed!
> Mayest thou never know
> A single day of peace!
> And even when thou dost go
> To kneel before the altar,
> Mayest thou feel forsaken,
> And bitterly regret
> The step which thou hast taken!

TO CURSE A WOMAN'S UNBORN CHILD
SIOUAN INDIAN SPELL

To cause an expectant mother's child to be born with loathsome qualities, feed her the flesh of a turtle along with the flesh of a porcupine. Her child will grow up to lazy and unproductive, and will never bring any fortunes to his family.

TO CAST AWAY SLANDER
POW-WOW CHARM

If you are calumniated or slandered to your very skin, to your very flesh, to your very bones, cast it back upon the false tongues. Take off your shirt and turn it wrong side out, and then run your two thumbs along your body, close under the ribs, starting at the pit of the heart down to the thighs.

 ## TO SILENCE GOSSIP
AMERICAN WITCH'S CHARM

To banish gossip or other words, explain as concisely as possible in writing what matter you need the spirits' help in silencing. Place this writing on parchment inside a small glass. Place a single sliver of ice on top of the paper, then break an egg (use white eggs only, not brown) over the ice. Bury as far away as possible.

COUNTER-Spells

AGAINST ONE WHO PRACTICES HOSTILE MAGIC
ANCIENT HINDU INCANTATION

To counter a curse from a hostile force, recite:

> The thousand-eyed curse having yoked his chariot has come hither, seeking out him who curses me, as a wolf the house of him who owns sheep.

> Avoid us, O curse, as a burning fire avoids a lake! Strike here he who curses us, as the lightning of heaven the tree!

> He who shall curse us when we do not curse, and he that shall curse us when we do curse, him do I hurl to death as a bone to a dog upon the ground.

AGAINST WITCHES
EUROPEAN MAGICIAN'S SPELL

To ward off witches, remember to purify thy home with the branches of cypress and of pine, then pronounce at midnight:

> Who art thou, O witch, who seekest me?
> Thou hast taken the road
> Thou hast come after me

Thou hast sought me continually for my
    destruction
Thou hast continually plotted evil against me
Thou hast encompassed me
Thou hast sought me out
Thou hast gone forth and followed my steps

But I, by the command of the Queen Ishtar
Am clothed in terror
Am armed in fierceness
Am arrayed with might and the Sword
I make thee tremble
I make thee run afraid
I drive thee out
I spy thee out

I cause thy name to be known among men
I cause thy house to be seen among men
I cause thy spells to be heard among men
I cause thy evil perfumes to be smelt among
    men
I unclothe thy wickedness and evil
And bring your sorceries to naught!

It is not I, but Nanakanisurra,
Mistress of Witches,
And the Queen of Heaven, Ishtar,
Who command thee!

THAT NO WITCH MAY LEAVE A CHURCH
GYPSY CHARM

So that no witch may leave a church, purchase a pair of new shoes, grease them on Saturday with grease on the outer sole, then put them on and walk to the church, and no witch can find the way out of the church without you proceeding before her.

TO KILL A WITCH WHO IS KILLING CATTLE
GYPSY CHARM

If a witch is found to be killing livestock, to effect her death perform this charm. Obtain a piece of the heart of the cattle that has been attacked, then take a little butter and fry the piece therein, as if preparing for eating. Then take three nails from the coffin of a corpse, and pierce with them the heart through and through. Piercing the heart and killing the witch are facts of the same moment. All will be correct at once.

TO MAKE A WITCH SICK
GYPSY CHARM

To burn a witch with pockmarks all over her body, take butter from the household larder, render it down in an iron pan until it boils, then take ivy or wintergreen and fry it. Take three nails from a coffin of a corpse and stick them in that sauce; carry the mass to a place where neither sun nor moon shines into and leave it there, and the witch will be sick for half of a year.

AGAINST FAIRY INFLUENCE
GAELIC SPELL

To protect oneself or one's home against fairy influence, call out:

> We accept their protection,
> We repudiate their evil tricks,
> May their backs be to us, their faces from us
> Through merit of the passion and death of our
>   Savior.

AGAINST HORDES OF DEMONS AND OTHER EVIL INFLUENCES
NECROMANCER'S SPELL

As a spell against demon hordes and other evil influences, pronounce:

> Arise! Arise! Go far away!
> Be shamed! Be shamed! Flee! Flee!
> Turn around, go, arise, and go far away!
> Your wickedness may rise to heaven like smoke!
>
> Arise and leave my body!
> From my body, depart in shame!
> From my body flee!
> Turn away from my body!
> Go away from my body!
> Do not return to my body!
> Do not come near my body!
> Do not approach my body!
> Do not throng around my body!
>
> Be commanded by Shammash the Mighty!
> Be commanded by Enki, Lord of All!
> Be commanded by Marduk, the Great
>   Magician of the Gods!
> Be commanded by the God of Fire, your
>   Destroyer!
> May you be held back from my body!

 ## AGAINST OMINOUS PIGEONS AND OWLS
ANCIENT HINDU INCANTATION

As a charm against ominous pigeons and owls, recite:

> Upon those persons yonder the winged missile
> shall fall! If the owl shrieks, futile shall this be,
> or if the pigeon takes his steps upon the fire!

> To thy two messengers, O Nirriti, who come
> here, dispatched or not dispatched, to our
> house, to the pigeon and to the owl, this shall
> be no place to step upon! He shall not fly hither
> to slaughter our men; to keep our men sound
> he shant settle here!

> Charm him very far away unto a distant
> region, that people shall behold him in Yama's
> house devoid of strength, that they shall behold
> him bereft of power!

AGAINST SORCERY
GYPSY CHARM

As a precaution against sorcery, take elm wood on a Good
Friday and cut the same while calling the three holiest
names. Cut chips of this wood from one to two inches in
length. Cut upon them three crosses. Wherever they are
placed, all sorcery will be banished.

TO REPEL SPELLS OR SORCERIES
ANCIENT HINDU INCANTATION

To repel spells or sorceries, recite:

> An eagle found thee out, a boar dug thee out
> with his snout. Seek thou, O plant, to injure
> him who seeks to injure us, strike down him
> that prepares spells against us!
>
> Strike down the wizards, strike down him that
> prepares spells against us; slay thou, moreover,
> O plant, him that seeks to injure us!
>
> Cutting out from the skin of the enemy as if
> from the skin of an antelope, do ye, O gods,
> fasten the spell upon him that prepares it, as
> one fastens an ornament!

Take hold of the hand and lead away the spell back to the spell caster! Place it in his very presence, so that it shall slay him who prepares the spell!

The spells shall take effect upon him who prepares the spells, the curse upon him who pronounces the curse! As a chariot with easygoing wheels, the spell shall turn back upon the spell caster!

Whether a woman or whether a man has prepared the spell for evil, we lead that spell to him as a horse with the halter.

Whether thou hast been prepared by the gods, or hast been prepared by men, we lead thee back with the help of Indra as an ally.

O Agni, gainer of battles, do thou gain the battles! With a counter-charm do we hurl back the spell upon him who prepares the spell.

Hold ready, O plant, thy weapon, and strike him, slay the very one who has cast the spell! We do not whet thee for the destruction of him who has not practiced the spell.

Go as a son to his father, bite like an adder that has been stepped upon. Return thou, O spell, to him who prepares the spell, as one who overcomes his fetters!

As the shy deer and the antelope go out to the mating buck, thus the spell shall reach him who prepares it!

Straighter than an arrow may the spell fly against him, O ye heaven and earth; may that spell take hold again of him who prepares it, as a hunter of his game!

Like fire the spell shall progress in the teeth of obstacles, like water along its course! As a chariot with easy-going wheels the spell shall turn back upon the spell caster!

TO BANISH SORCERERS AND DEMONS
ANCIENT HINDU INCANTATION

As a charm against sorcerers and demons, recite:

May this oblation carry hither the sorcerers, as a river carries foam! The man or the woman who has performed this sorcery, that person shall here proclaim himself!

This vaunting sorcerer has come hither: receive him with alacrity! O Brihaspati, put him into subjection; O Agni and Soma, pierce him through!

Slay the offspring of the sorcerer, O soma-
drinking Indra, and him! Make drop out the
farther and the nearer eye of the braggart!

Wherever, O Agni Gâtavedas, thou perceivest
the brood of these hidden devourers, do thou,
mightily strengthened by our charm, slay them:
slay their brood, O Agni, piercing them a
hundredfold!

TO DRIVE AWAY SPIRITS HAUNTING A HOUSE
EUROPEAN WITCH'S CHARM

To drive away spirits that haunt a home, hang in every
corner of your house this sentence, written upon virgin
parchment:

> *Omnis spiritus laudet Dominum: Mosen habent and*
> *prophetas: Exurgat Deus et dissipentur inimici ejus.*

TO RESTORE A BEING OR BEAST WHO HAS BEEN ATTACKED BY EVIL SPIRITS
GYPSY SPELL

To restore a being or beast who has been attacked by evil spirits, pronounce three times:

> Thou arch-sorcerer, thou has attacked [Name];
> let that witchcraft recede from him into thy
> marrow and into thy bone, let it be returned
> unto thee. I exorcise thee for the sake of the five
> wounds of Jesus, thou evil spirit, and conjure
> thee for the five wounds of Jesus of this flesh,
> marrow, and bone; I exorcise thee for the sake
> of the five wounds of Jesus, at this very hour
> restore to health again [Name], in the name
> of God the Father, God the Son, and God the
> Holy Spirit.

TO EXORCISE A POSSESSING SPIRIT
NECROMANCER'S SPELL

This exorcism against a possessing spirit is to be said when the body of possessed is distant or when secrecy must be maintained. Within thy Circle, recite:

> The wicked God
> The wicked Demon
> The Demon of the Desert

The Demon of the Mountain
The Demon of the Sea
The Demon of the Marsh

The Wicked Genius
The Enormous Larvae
The Wicked Winds
The Demon that seizeth the body
The Demon that rendeth the body
Spirit of the Sky, remember!
Spirit of the Earth, remember!

The Demon that seizeth man
The Gigim who worketh Evil
The Spawn of the wicked Demon
Spirit of the Sky, remember!
Spirit of the Earth, remember!

He who forges images
He who casts spells
The Evil Angel
The Evil Eye
The Evil Mouth
The Evil Tongue
The Evil Lip
The Most Perfect Sorcery
Spirit of the Sky, remember!
Spirit of the Earth, remember!

Ninnkigal, Wife of Ninnazu
May she cause him to turn his face toward the

Place where she is!
May the wicked Demons depart!
May they seize one another!
May they feed on one another's bones!
Spirit of the Sky, remember!
Spirit of the Earth, remember!

TO EXORCISE A BEWITCHED CHILD
GYPSY SPELL

When a child is bewitched, stand with the child toward
the morning sun, and speak:

> Be welcome in God's name and sunshine, from
> whence didst brightly beam, aid me and my
> dear child and feign my songs serenely stream.
>
> To God the Father sound my praise, help praise
> the Holy Ghost that he restore my child to
> health, I praise the heavenly host.

AGAINST BAD MEN AND EVIL SPIRITS THAT TORMENT YOUNG AND OLD
POW-WOW CHARM

To protect and free all persons and animals against bad
men and evil spirits that nightly torment old and young
people, write this and place it on the bedstead:

Trotter Head, I forbid thee my house and premises; I forbid thee my horse and cow-stable; I forbid thee my bedstead, that thou mayest not breathe upon me; breathe into some other house, until thou hast ascended every hill, until thou hast counted every fence-post, and until thou hast crossed every water. And thus dear day may come again into my house, in the name of God the Father, the Son, and the Holy Ghost. Amen.

AGAINST EVIL DREAMS
ANCIENT HINDU INCANTATION

To rid one of evil dreams, recite:

Thou who art neither alive nor dead, the immortal child of the gods art thou, O Sleep! Varunânî is thy mother, Yama, thy father; Araru is thy name.

We know, O Sleep, thy birth, thou art the son of the divine women-folk, the instrument of Yama! Thou art the ender, thou art death! Thus do we know thee, O Sleep: do thou, O Sleep, protect us from evil dreams!

As one pays off a sixteenth, an eighth, or an entire debt, thus do we transfer every evil dream upon our enemy.

TO COUNTERACT THE EVIL EYE
GAELIC INCANTATION

To counteract the Evil Eye, recite:

> An eye covered thee,
> A mouth spoke thee,
> A heart envied thee,
> A mind desired thee.
>
> Four made thee thy cross,
> Man and wife,
> Youth and maid;
> Three will send to
>   thwart them,
> Father,
> Son,
> Spirit Holy.
>
> I appeal to Mary,
> Aidful mother of men,
> I appeal to Bride,
> Foster-mother of Christ
>   omnipotent,
> I appeal to Columba,
> Apostle of shore and sea,
> And I appeal to heaven,
> To all saints and angels that be above.
>
> If it be a man that has done thee harm,
> With evil eye,

With evil wish,
With evil passion,

Mayest thou cast off each ill,
Every malignity;
Every malice,
Every harassment,
And mayest thou be well forever,
While this thread
Goes round thee,
In honor of God and of Jesus,
And of the Spirit of balm everlasting.

TO KEEP THE EVIL EYE AWAY FROM SOMEONE ELSE'S CHILD

GYPSY POTION

To keep the Evil Eye from someone else's child, fill a jar with water from a stream. It must be taken with, not against, the current as it runs. In it, place seven coals, seven handfuls of meal, and seven cloves of garlic, then place on a fire. When the water begins to boil, stir it with a three-forked twig while repeating:

Evil eyes look on thee,
May they here extinguished be
And then seven ravens
Pluck out the evil eyes.

Evil eyes now look on thee.
May they soon extinguished be!
Much dust in the eyes,
Thence may they become blind,
Evil eyes now look on thee;

May they soon extinguished be!

May they burn, may they burn
In the fire of God!

Sprinkle the water in the bed linens of the child and on her clothing.

 ## TO PREVENT FIREARMS FROM BEING BEWITCHED
GYPSY CHARM

Take nine blades of straw from under a sow while she is nursing young pigs, therefrom put nine knots into the shaft and insert them between the two barrel loops, and such a gun cannot be bewitched.

LUCK AND
FORTUNE

 **FOR LASTING LIFE**
GAELIC INCANTATION

For a long and lasting life, recite:

> I place the charm on thy body,
> And on thy prosperity,
> The charm of the God of Life
> For thy protection.

> The charm that Bride of the King
> Put round the fair neck of Dornghil,
> The charm that Mary put about her Son,
> Between sole and throat,
> Between pap and knee,
> Between back and breast,
> Between chest and sole,
> Between eye and hair.

> The glove of Michael on thy side,
> The shield of Michael on thy shoulder,
> There is not one between heaven and earth
> Who can overcome the King of Grace.

> No spear shall rive thee,
> No sea shall drown thee,
> No woman shall wile thee,
> No man shall wound thee.

The mantle of Christ Himself about thee,
The shadow of Christ Himself above thee,
From the crown of thy head
To the soles of thy feet.
The char of God is on thee now,
Thou shall never know disgrace nor calamity.

Thou shall go forth in the name of thy King,
Thou shall come in the name of thy Chief,
To the God of life thou now belongest wholly,
And to all the Powers together.

I place this charm early on Monday,
In passage hard, brambly, thorny,
Go thou out with the charm about thy body,
And be not the least fear upon thee.

Thou shall ascend the crest of the hill
Protected, thou shall be behind thee,
Thou art the calm swan in battle,
Preserved, thou shall be amidst the slaughter,
Stand thou canst against five hundred,
And thine oppressors shall be seized.

The charm of God about thee!
The arm of God above thee!

TO DREAM PLEASANT DREAMS
AMERICAN WITCH'S SPELL

To dream pleasant dreams while you rest, place lavender near your beside. Sleep with your arms outstretched (preferably on your back) and give yourself to sleep while taking deep breaths and repeating in your mind:

>Dreams be kind
>Dreams be wise
>Dreams be mine
>Dreams be mind.

TO MAKE ONESELF HAPPY
AMERICAN WITCH'S SPELL

To bring about happiness in oneself, recite as many times as necessary:

>I have word for you,
>For you, Sad-Heart,
>And pray you keep it till the dawn come true,
>And sorrow part.

>I never bid you doff
>A single care:
>But ever till tomorrow, O, put off—
>Put off Despair!

THAT ONE WILL COME INTO THE POSSESSION OF MONEY
AMERICAN MAGICIAN'S CHARM

To come into the possession of money, take the eggs of a swallow, boil them, return them to the nest, and if the old swallow brings a root to the nest, take it, put it into your purse or carry it in your pocket, and be happy.

TO HAVE MONEY ALWAYS
GAELIC CHARM

To have money always, first kill a black rooster. Then, after nightfall, go to the meeting of three crossroads where a murderer is buried. Throw the dead bird over your left shoulder then and there, in the name of the devil, holding a piece of money in your hand all the while. And ever after, no matter what you spend, you will always find the same piece of money undiminished in your pocket.

⊙⊙ TO FIND TREASURE HIDDEN BY THE SPIRITS
⊙⊙ EUROPEAN MAGICIAN'S CHARM

The following instructions are given to render thyself master of a treasure possessed by the Spirits. The Earth is inhabited by a great number of Celestial Beings and Spirits who, by their subtlety and prevision, know the places wherein treasures are hidden. It often happeneth that those men who undertake a search for these said treasures are sometimes put to death by the aforesaid Spirits, but if thou shall have the good fortune to be familiar with kind Spirits, thou shall be able, by means of what I have taught thee, to make them submit unto thine orders. They will be happy to give thee, and to make thee partaker in that which they uselessly possess, provided that thine object and end shall be to make a good use thereof.

On a Sunday before sunrise, between the 10th of July and the 20th of August, when the moon is in the Sign of the Lion, thou shall go unto the place where thou shall know either by interrogation of the Intelligences or otherwise, that there is a treasure; there thou shall describe a Circle of sufficient size wherein to open up the earth, as the nature of the ground will allow; thrice during the day shall thou cense it with the incense proper for the day, after which being clothed in the raiment proper for the Operation thou shall suspend in some way by a machine immediately above the opening a lamp, whose oil should be mingled with the fat of a man who has died in the month of July, and the wick being made from the cloth wherein he has been buried. Thou shall set the hole-diggers to work in safety, warning them not to be at all disturbed at the Spectres which they will see, but to work away boldly. In case they cannot finish the work in a single day, every time they shall have to leave it thou shall cause them to put a covering of wood over the opening, and above the covering about six inches of earth; and thus shall thou continue unto the end, after which thou shall repeat:

> Adonai, Elohim, El, Eheieh, Asher Eheih,
> Prince of Princes, Existence of Existences, have
> mercy upon me, and cast Thine eyes upon
> Thy servant, [Name], who invokes Thee most
> devoutedly, and supplicates Thee by Thy Holy
> and tremendous Name Tetragrammaton to
> be propitious, and to order Thine Angels and
> Spirits to come and take up their abode in this
> place; O ye Angels and Spirits of the Stars, O
> all ye Angels and Elementary Spirits, O all ye
> Spirits present before the Face of God, I the
> Minister and faithful Servant of the Most High
> conjure ye, let God Himself, the Existence of

Existences, conjure ye to come and be present
at this Operation, I, the Servant of God, most
humbly entreat ye. Amen.

Having then caused the workmen to fill in the hole, thou
shall license the Spirits to depart, thanking them for the
favor they have shown unto thee, and saying:

O ye good and happy Spirits, we thank ye for
the benefits which we have just received from
your liberal bounty; depart ye in peace to gov-
ern the Element which God hath destined for
your habitation. Amen.

TO WIN EVERY GAME OF CARDS
POW-WOW CHARM

Tie the heart of a bat with a red silken string to your right
arm, and you will win every game of cards you play.

TO HAVE SUCCESS IN GAMBLING
ANCIENT HINDU INCANTATION

To have success in the game of dice or other games of chance, recite:

> The successful, victorious, skillfully gaming Apsarâ, that Apsarâ who makes the winnings in the game of dice, do I call hither.

> The skillfully gaming Apsarâ who sweeps and heaps up the stakes, that Apsarâ, who takes the winnings in the game of dice, do I call hither.

> May she, who dances about with the dice, when she takes the stakes from the game of dice, when she desires to win for us, obtain the advantage by her magic! May she come to us full of abundance! Let them not win this wealth of ours!

> The Apsarâs who rejoice in dice, who carry grief and wrath—that joyful and exulting Apsarâ, do I call hither!

TO WIN THE LOTTERY
AMERICAN WITCH'S INCANTATION

To win any time one plays the lottery, perform the following: Lying down, recite three times the following prayer, then write it on virgin parchment and place under your pillow:

> *Domine Jesu Christe, qui dixisti ego sum via, veritas et vita, ecce enim vertatem dilexisti, incerta et occulta sapientiae tuae mainfestasti mihi, adhuc quae reveles in hac nocte sicut ita revelatum fuit parvulis solis, incongnita et ventura unique alia me doceas, ut possim omnia cognoscere, si et si sit; ita monstra mihi montem ornatum omni nivo bono, pulchrum et gratum pomarium, aut quondam rem gratam, sin autem minstra mihi ignem ardentem, vel aquarum currentem vel aliam quamcumque rem quae Domino placeat, et vel Angeli Ariel, Rubiel et Barachiel sitis mihi multum amatores et factores ad opus istud obtinendum quod cupio scire, videre cognoscere et praevidere per illum Deum qui venturus est judicare vivos et mortuos, et saeculum per ignem. Amen.*

During sleep a dream will come that will tell you the hour that you must get your ticket.

TO GAIN STRENGTH
AMERICAN WITCH'S SPELL

To gain strength, repeat this spell in the sun:

I reach my arms up, to the sky,
And golden vine on vine
Of sunlight showered wild and high,
Around my brows I twine.

I wreathe, I wind it everywhere,
The burning radiancy
Of brightness that no eye may dare,
To be the strength of me.

Come, redness of the crystalline,
Come green, come hither blue
And violet—all alive within,
For I have need of you.

Come honey-hue and flush of gold,
And through the pallor run,
With pulse on pulse of manifold
New largess of the Sun!

O steep the silence till it sing!
O glories from the height,
Come down, where I am garlanding
With light, a child of light!

FOR GOOD LUCK WHILE HUNTING
CHEROKEE SHAMAN'S CHANT

To have good luck at the hunt, repeat:

> Give me the wind. Give me the breeze. *Yû!* O
> Great Terrestrial Hunter, I come to the edge of
> your spittle where you repose. Let your stom-
> ach cover itself; let it be covered with leaves.
> Let it cover itself at a single bend, and may you
> never be satisfied.

> And you, O Ancient Red, may you hover above
> my breast while I sleep. Now let good dreams
> develop; let my experiences be propitious. Ha!
> Now let my little trails be directed, as they lie
> down in various directions. Let the leaves be
> covered with the clotted blood, and may it
> never cease to be so. The Water and the Fire
> shall bury it in your stomach. *Yû!*

 ## TO ENCHANT FIREARMS
AMERICAN WITCH'S SPELL

To enchant a firearm, say:

> God has a share in it and the devil has the exit.

And when you fire, say the following while crossing your
left leg over your right:

> *Non tradas Dominum nostrum Jesum Christum.*
> *Mathon.* Amen.

TO FIND GAINFUL EMPLOYMENT
HOODOO CHARM

This spell is to be used only as a last resort if one cannot find gainful employment. After inquiring after an
opportunity, inscribe a green candle with the name of
the proprietor using the eye of a needle. On the side of a
red candle, draw three arrows running from the bottom
toward the wick, representing Tiwaz.

Burn both candles side-by-side after dark each night
at the same time, until your inquiries have been answered.
While the candles are burning, leave a small container of
milk on your doorstep as an offering. After envisioning
your desired outcome, snuff the candles (do not blow out)
and think only serious thoughts until bedtime.

TO BE LUCKY IN EVERY ENTERPRISE
AMERICAN WITCH'S POTION

To be lucky in every enterprise, take a green frog and cut
off its head and its four feet. Then on a Friday with a full
moon, put them in an elder-tree and keep them there for
twenty-one days, removing them on the twenty-first day
precisely at midnight.

Then expose the parts of the frog to the light of the moon for three nights. Afterward, dry the frog parts in an earthenware pot that has never been used. Take the dried frog parts and grind them to a powder. Mix the powder in equal measure with crushed earthenware taken from a cemetery—if possible, from the grave of someone in your family.

Carry the powder mixture with you. It will help you succeed in any undertaking.

 **FOR PROSPERITY IN BUSINESS**
HOODOO POTION

Run a bath and add five sprigs of basil and three lodestones or magnets. Enter the bath and sit for at least twenty minutes. Then use this water to soak the entrance to where your business takes place. Place the lodestones in a triangle around where you are to perform your work. Repeat when energy becomes stagnant.

TO MAKE SOMEONE LEAVE THEIR JOB SO YOU MAY TAKE IT
AMERICAN WITCH'S CHARM

Place five nails that your rival has touched in a jar with water from the earth. Place the jar in a dark area until rust forms. Rub the water from the jar around the workplace of your rival before each day of work. If he doesn't leave on his own accord, his cursed work will cause him to be terminated.

TO WIN A LAWSUIT
POW-WOW CHARM

If one has to settle a just claim by way of a lawsuit, let him take some of the largest kind of sage and write the name of the twelve apostles on the leaves and put them in his shoes before entering the courthouse, and he shall certainly gain the suit.

TO GET A JUDGE TO FAVOR YOU
POW-WOW SPELL

To retain favor in court and council, first carry these words with you, written on paper, and then pronounce them when approaching the court:

> I, [Name], appear before the house of the Judge. Three dead men look out of the window; one having no tongue; the other having no lungs; and the third being sick, blind, and dumb.

This is intended to be used when you are standing before a court in your right, and the judge is not favorably disposed toward you.

LOVE AND
MATCHMAKING

TO SEE ONE'S MARITAL FUTURE
AMERICAN MAGICIAN'S CHARM

If you wish to know what man you will wed, buy a ring; it matters not it being gold, so as it has the semblance of a wedding ring; and it is best to try this charm on your own birthday. Pay for your ring with some small bill, for whatever change you receive you must give to the first beggar you meet in the street; and, if no one asks alms of you, give it to some poor person—for you need not (alas!) go far before you find one to whom your charity will be acceptable; carefully note what they say in return, such as "God bless you," or wishing you luck and prosperity, as is usual. When you get home, write what was said down on a sheet of paper, at each of the four corners, and in the middle, put the two first letters of your name, your age, and the letters of the planets then reigning as morning and evening stars.

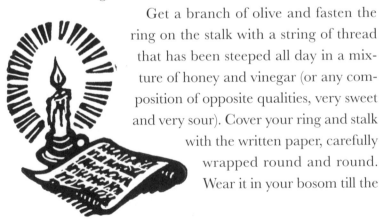

Get a branch of olive and fasten the ring on the stalk with a string of thread that has been steeped all day in a mixture of honey and vinegar (or any composition of opposite qualities, very sweet and very sour). Cover your ring and stalk with the written paper, carefully wrapped round and round. Wear it in your bosom till the ninth hour of the night; then repair to the next church-yard and bury the charm in the grave of a young man who died unmarried; and, while you are so doing, repeat the letters of your own Christian name three times backwards.

Return home, and keep as silent as possible till you go to bed, which must be done before eleven; put a light in your chimney, or some safe place; and, before midnight, or just about that time, your husband that is to be will present himself at the foot of the bed, but will presently disappear. If you are not to marry, none will come, and, in that case, if you dream before morning of children, it shows that you will have them unmarried; and if you dream of crowds of men, beware of prostitution.

 ## FOR THREE MAIDENS TO DISCERN WHOM THEY SHALL MARRY
AMERICAN WITCH'S CHARM

To discern whom they shall marry, three young maidens should join together in making a long chain—about a yard will do—of Christmas juniper and mistletoe berries, and, at the end of every link, put an oak acorn. Exactly before midnight let them assemble in a room by themselves, where no one can disturb them; leave a window open, and take the key out of the keyhole and hang it over the chimney-piece; have a good fire, and place in the midst of it a long, thinnish log of wood, well-sprinkled with oil, salt, and fresh mold; then wrap the chain round it, each maiden having an equal share in the business; then sit down, and on your left knee let each fair one have a prayer-book opened at the matrimonial service. Just as the last acorn is burned, the future husband will cross the room; each one will see her own proper spouse, but he will be invisible to the rest of the wakeful virgins. Those who are not to be wed will see a coffin, or some misshapen form, cross the room. This must be done either on a Wednesday or Friday night, but no other.

 ## TO SEE A VISAGE OF ONE'S FUTURE HUSBAND

AMERICAN MAGICIAN'S CHARM

This charm to see a visage of your future husband is to be attempted on the 21st of January, St. Agnes' Day. You must prepare yourself by a twenty-fours' fast, touching nothing but pure spring water, beginning at midnight on the 20th to the same again on the 21st. Then go to bed. Mind you, sleep by yourself; and do not mention what you are trying to anyone, or it will break the spell; go to rest on your left side, and repeat these lines three times:

> Saint Agnes be a friend to me,
> In the gift I ask of thee;
> Let me this night my husband see.

And you will dream of your future spouse; if you see more men than one in your dream, you will wed two or three times; but if you sleep and dream not, you will never marry.

 ## TO LEARN THE FIRST INITIAL OF ONE'S INTENDED
GAELIC CHARM

Pare an apple so that the peel remains in one long piece. Swing this around your head three times and throw it on the floor. The letter it forms will be the initial of your intended sweetheart's name.

TO KNOW THE NAME OF THE PERSON WHOM ONE IS TO MARRY
TUSCAN WITCH'S CHARM

Take a stone of rather large size, as round as you can get it, and go by night to a covered well; it is best if it were in the middle of some field or garden. And just as the clock strikes one, cast the stone, *con gran fracasso*—with as much noise as you can make—into the water.

Then listen with care to hear the sound produced by the fall of the stone. Although it may be a little obscure or confused, and not always very intelligible, with a little patience and attention one can detect in the sound that the stone makes in the water the name of the person whom one is to marry.

TO KNOW WHAT FORTUNE ONE'S FUTURE HUSBAND SHALL HAVE
AMERICAN MAGICIAN'S CHARM

Take a walnut, a hazelnut, and nutmeg; grate them together; and mix them with butter and sugar. Make them up into small pills, of which exactly nine must be taken upon going to bed; and according to your dreams, so will be the state of the person you will marry. If he is to be a gentleman, your dream will be of riches; if a clergyman, of white linen; if a lawyer, of darkness; if a tradesman, of cold noises and tumults; if a soldier or sailor, of thunder and lightning; if a servant, of rain.

TO AROUSE THE PASSIONATE LOVE OF A MAN
ANCIENT HINDU INCANTATION

To arouse the passionate love of a man, go to a location where you can espy him but he cannot espy you. Once there, recite:

> This yearning love comes from the Apsaras, the victorious, imbued with victory. Ye gods, send forth the yearning love: May yonder man burn after me!
>
> My wish is: He shall long for me, devoted he shall long for me! Ye gods, send forth the yearning love: May yonder man burn after me!
>
> That yonder man shall long for me, but I for him nevermore, ye gods, send forth the yearning love: May yonder man burn after me!
>
> Do ye, O Maruts, intoxicate him with love; do thou, O mid-air, intoxicate him; do thou, O Agni, intoxicate him! May yonder man burn after me!

TO AROUSE THE PASSIONATE LOVE OF A WOMAN
ANCIENT HINDU INCANTATION

To arouse the passionate love of a woman, recite:

> May Love, the disquieter, disquiet thee; do not hold out upon thy bed! With the terrible arrow of Kâma do I pierce thee in the heart.

> The arrow, winged with longing, barbed with love, whose shaft is undeviating desire, with that, well-aimed, Kâma shall pierce thee in the heart!

> With that well-aimed arrow of Kâma which parches the spleen, whose plume flies forward, which burns up, do I pierce thee in the heart.

> Consumed by burning ardor, with parched mouth, do thou come to me, pliant, thy pride laid aside, mine alone, speaking sweetly and to me devoted!

> I drive thee with a goad from thy mother and thy father, so that thou shall be in my power, shall come up to my wish.

> All her thoughts do ye, O Mitra and Varuna, drive out of her! Then, having deprived her of her will, put her into my power alone!

 TO INCREASE ONE'S BEAUTY
ANCIENT ASIATIC INCANTATION

To increase one's beauty and thereby increase one's chances of finding love, recite to the Gods:

> The Aarthi, that Demon that is causing my ugliness, I cast thee out. Varuna, Mitra, remove a perceived lack of grace. Aryaman, protect my hands. Savitr, banish all ugliness! Let all unwelcome aspects of mind, body, and spirit disappear. Let me be happy, as it was why I was created. Drive away even the smallest blemish.

TO PROMOTE THE GROWTH OF HAIR
ANCIENT HINDU INCANTATION

To promote the growth of hair, recite:

> Of these three Earths, our Earth verily is the highest. From the surface of these I have now plucked a remedy.
>
> Thou art the most excellent of remedies, the best of plants, as Soma (the moon) is the lord of the watchers of the night, as Varuna is king among the gods.
>
> O ye wealthy, irresistible plants, ye do generously bestow benefits. And ye strengthen the hair, and, moreover, promote its increase.

TO MAKE SOMEONE A GOOD DANCER
ESKIMO SHAMAN'S CHANT

To make a person dance well, sing:

> Oh woman! Oh being! I will teach thee a song
> for one destined for getting down.
>
> One that will make you itch to trample it down.
>
> Sing to me when you are stamping the ground.
> I will dance with you.
> There, woman, scratch it, give it the cramps!

TO MAKE A WOMAN MOVED TO LOVE
GYPSY SPELL

To make a woman moved to love, her lover must take a blade of grass in his mouth, and turning to the East and the West, say:

> Where the sun goes up
> Shall my love be by me
> Where the sun goes down
> There by her I'll be.

Then the blade of grass should be cut up into pieces and mingled with some food, which the girl must eat, and if she swallows the least bit of the grass, she will be *gewogen* und *treugesinnt*—moved to love and truehearted.

TO ENCHANT A WOMAN INTO LOVE
GYPSY CHARM

On Friday early as may be,
Take the fairest apple from a tree,
Then in thy blood on paper white
Thy own name and thy true love's write,
That apple thou in two shall cut,
And for its cure that paper put,
With two sharp pins of myrtle wood
Join the halves till it seem good,
In the oven let it dry,
And wrapped in leaves of myrtle lie,
Under the pillow of thy dear,
Yet let it be unknown to her
And if it a secret be
She soon will show her love for thee.

TO MAKE A MAIDEN FALL IN LOVE
ANCIENT MACEDONIAN CHARM

To make a maiden fall in love, take three live fishes and place them in a row upon a gridiron over a fire. While the fishes are cooking, hit them in turns with two small sticks, repeating this incantation:

> As these fishes are panting, even so may the
> maiden whom I love pant with longing.

When they are thoroughly charred, pound them into a mortar and reduce them to fine powder, out of which you'll concoct a potion. Then endeavor to make the maid drink of it.

FOR TRUE LOVE
ANCIENT JEWISH CHARM

Take a live mole (a male for a man, a female for a woman) and strike it on its right foot, and it will bring you true love.

TO CAUSE SOMEONE TO FALL IN LOVE
ANCIENT JEWISH CHARM

If an all-black hen that has never laid an egg before lays an egg on Thursday, take the egg on Thursday night after sunset and bury it at a crossroads. And on Tuesday, take the egg from there after sunset. Then trade this egg for a mirror, and bury the mirror at the same crossroads after sunset in the name òf Lady Venus and say,

> Here I bury this mirror in the love that Lady
> Venus has for Tannhaeuser.

Let it lie there for three days, and take it out; and whoever looks into it will love you.

TO MAKE ONE'S SWEETHEART RAVENOUS
AMERICAN MAGICIAN'S CHARM

When you wish that your sweetheart shall not deny you, take the turtle-dove tongue into your mouth and kiss her, and she will accept your suit. Or: Take salt, cheese, and flour; mix them together; and put it into her room; and she will have no rest until she sees you.

TO MAKE A WOMAN FOLLOW
GAELIC CHARM

To make a woman follow, keep a sprig of mint in your hand till the herb grows moist and warm, then take hold of the hand of the woman you love, and she will follow you as long as the two hands close over the herb. No invocation is necessary, but silence must be kept between the two parties for ten minutes, to give the charm time to work with due efficacy.

TO CAUSE SOMEONE TO SEEK YOU OUT
EUROPEAN MAGICIAN'S CHARM

If a distance has passed between you and a person and you desire her presence, practice this charm, which can only be performed when a star is observed between eleven o'clock and midnight. Before beginning, do as follows: Take a virgin parchment. Write thereon her name whose presence you desire. On the other side inscribe these names:

Melchidael, Bareschas.

Then place your parchment on the earth, with the person's name against the ground. Set your right foot above it while your left knee is bent to the earth. In this position observe the brightest star in the firmament, holding in your right hand a taper of white wax large enough to last for an hour, and recite the following conjuration:

> I salute and conjure you, O beautiful Moon, O beautiful Star, O bright light, which I hold in my hand! By the air that I breathe, by the breath that is within me, by the earth that I touch, I conjure you, and by all the names of the spirits who are princes residing in you; I conjure you again by all the Divine Names of God, that you send down to obsess, torment, and harass the body, spirit, soul, and five senses of the nature of [Name of whom thy seek], whose name is written here below, in such a way that she shall come unto me and accomplish my will. Go then, promptly; go, Melchidael, Bareschas, Zazel, Firiel, Malcha, and all those who are without you. I conjure you by the great living God to accomplish my will, and I, [Name], do promise to satisfy you duly.

Having thrice pronounced this conjuration, place the wax taper on the parchment and let it burn. Take the parchment on the morrow, put it in your left shoe, and there leave it until the person for whom you have operated seeks you out.

TO LOSE ONE'S INFATUATION WITH AN ILLICIT LOVE
GYPSY SPELL

If one has been infatuated by an illicit love, such a person must put a pair of shoes on and walk therein until his feet perspire; he must walk fast so that his feet do not smell badly. Then he must take off the right shoe, drink some beer or wine out of this shoe, and from that moment he shall lose all affection for her.

TO STOP AN INFATUATION
GYPSY SPELL

When you have lost your manhood due to being infatuated and bewitched by a woman so that you cannot love any other, take the blood of a buck and grease your head therewith, and you will soon be all right again.

FOR THE LOSING OF A MAN
ANCIENT MACEDONIAN CHARM

For the losing of a man: Write these words on a piece of bread, and give it to him to eat:

Akoel, eisvil, ampelouras, perimarias, kamenanton,
ektilen, ekpeilen, vriskadedeos, dedeousa.

TO VANQUISH A MAN
GYPSY SPELL

To vanquish a man, repeat thrice:

> I, [Name], will breathe on thee, three drops
> of blood I draw from thee. The first from thy
> heart, the other from thy liver, the third from
> thy vigorous life. By this I take all thy strength,
> and thou losest the strife.

TO DISCOVER IF A LOVER
HAS BEEN FAITHFUL
TUSCAN WITCH'S CHARM

To determine if a lover is faithful, take a snail or slug, such as are in gardens and which leave a streak as of silver behind them. Take one of these and a vase, and much ivy and vine leaves and calamint, and arrange the vase on a tree like a reversed umbrella, and within it put two portraits—that of the lover and of the lady—that is, of the

one whom you suspect he is unfaithful with. Place one on one side of the vase, one on the other, and put within the snail, and cover the vase with a white cloth. Leave it there for three days, having first said:

> In the name of the Father,
> And of the Son,
> And of the Evil Spirit,
> May they declare to me the truth
> If my husband or lover
> Has another love?

Then after three days examine whether the snail has gone to the picture of the man or the woman. If it be on the former, then the lover is faithful; but if on the woman, it is a sign that he is unfaithful.

 ## TO MAKE A LOVER COME BACK
AMERICAN MAGICIAN'S CHARM

If a maid wishes to see her lover, let her use the following method: Prick the third or wedding finger of your left hand with a sharp needle (beware a pin), and with the blood, write your own and your lover's name on a piece of clean writing paper, in as small a compass as you can, and encircle it with three round rings of the same crimson stream. Fold it up, and exactly at the ninth hour of the evening, bury it with your own hand in the earth, and tell no one. Your lover will hasten to you as soon as possible, and he will not be able to rest until he sees you, and (if you have quarreled) to make up. A young man may also try this charm, only instead of the wedding finger let him pierce the left thumb.

TO DISCERN IF A LOVE LETTER IS TRUE, AND THE FUTURE OF ITS WRITER
AMERICAN MAGICIAN'S CHARM

On receiving a love letter that has any particular declaration in it, lay it wide open; then fold it in nine folds; pin it next to your heart; and thus wear it till bedtime. Then place it in your left-hand glove, and lay it under your head. If you dream of gold, diamonds, or any other costly gem, your lover is true and means what he says; if of white linen, washing, or graves, you will lose him by death; and if of flowers, he will prove false. If you dream of his saluting you, he means not what he professes and will draw you into a snare. If you dream of castles or a clear sky, there is no deceit and you will prosper; trees in blossom denote children; and water shows that your lover is faithful but that you will go through severe poverty for some time, though all may end well.

TO GET A WOMAN TO ACCEPT A MARRIAGE PROPOSAL
EUROPEAN WITCH'S SPELL

To get a woman to accept your marriage proposal, take a gold ring that is studded with a small diamond and that has not been worn by anyone. Wrap it in a piece of green fabric, and for nine days and nine nights wear it against your heart. On the ninth day, before the sun rises, have the word "Scheva" engraved inside the ring by one who is a new engraver. Obtain three hairs from the person whom you want to love you, and tie them together with three of your own around the ring while saying:

> Body, that you could love me, that your desires could be as passionate as mine, by Scheva's most potent virtue.

Then wrap the ring in a piece of silk, and wear it against your heart for another six days. On the seventh day, fast. Before you have eaten, unwrap the ring and give it to the person you desire to love you.

If your ring is accepted, then you can be certain to be loved by that person. If the ring is refused, rest assured that the heart of that person belongs to another and in that case, you should seek your fortune elsewhere.

FOR THE OBTAINING OF A HUSBAND
ANCIENT HINDU INCANTATION

For the obtaining of a husband, recite:

> May, O Agni, a suitor after our own heart come to us, may he come to this maiden with our fortune! May she, agreeable to suitors, charming at festivals, promptly obtain happiness through a husband!

> Agreeable to Soma, agreeable to Brahma, arranged by Aryaman, with the unfailing certainty of god Dhâtar, do I bestow upon thee good fortune, the acquisition of a husband.

> This woman shall obtain a husband, since king Soma makes her lovely! May she, begetting sons, become a queen; may she, going to her husband, shine in loveliness!

> As this comfortable cave, O Maghavan, furnishing a safe abode, hath become pleasing to animals, thus may this woman be a favorite of Bhaga, beloved, not at odds with her husband!

> Do thou ascend the full, inexhaustible ship of fortune; upon this bring hither the suitor who shall be agreeable to thee!

> Bring hither by thy shouts, O lord of wealth, the suitor, bend his mind towards her; turn

thou the right side of every agreeable suitor towards her!

This gold and bdellium, this balsam, and fortune, too; these have prepared thee for husbands, that thou mayest obtain the one that is agreeable.

Hither to thee Savitar shall lead the husband that is agreeable! Do thou, O herb, bestow him upon her!

FOR THE OBTAINING OF A WIFE
ANCIENT HINDU INCANTATION

For the obtaining of a wife, recite:

I call the name of him who comes here, who hath come here, and is arriving; I crave the name of Indra, Vritra's slayer, the Visava, of hundredfold strength.

The road by which the Asvins carried away as a bride Sûryâ, Savitar's daughter, "by that road," Bhaga told me, "thou shall bring here a wife!"

With thy wealth-procuring, great, golden hook, O Indra, husband of Sakî, procure a wife for me, who desireth a wife!

TO KNOW HOW SOON ONE SHALL BE MARRIED

AMERICAN MAGICIAN'S CHARM

To know how soon you shall be married, get a green pea-pod in which there are exactly nine peas; hang it over the door; and then take notice of the next person who comes in who is not of the family, nor of the same sex as yourself; and if it proves to be an unmarried individual, you will certainly be married within that year.

THAT YOUR INTENDED WIFE WILL LOVE YOU
AMERICAN MAGICIAN'S CHARM

To cause your intended wife to love you, take feathers from a rooster's tail, and press them three times into her hand. Or, take a turtle-dove tongue into your mouth, talk to your friend agreeably, then kiss your intended and she will love you so clearly that she cannot love another.

 ## TO TEST IF A PERSON IS CHASTE
GYPSY CHARM

If you need to know if a person is chaste, the sap of a radish squeezed into her hand will prove what you wish to know. If she does not fumble or grabble, she is all right.

FOR SEEING THE FUTURE OF YOUR MARRIAGE
AMERICAN MAGICIAN'S POTION

To see the future of your marriage, perform the following on the third night of a new moon: Take a teaspoonful of brandy, rum, gin, wine, and the oil of amber, a tablespoonful of cream, and three of spring water; drink it as you get into bed. Recite:

> This mixture of love I take for my potion,
> That I of my destiny may have a notion;
> Cupid befriend me, new moon be kind,
> And show unto me that fate that's designed.

You will dream of drink, and, according to the quality or manner of it being presented, you may tell the condition to which you will rise or fall by marriage. If you dream of water, you will live in poverty; Champagne or spirits, prosperity. If you dream of drinking too much you will fall, at a future period, into that sad error yourself, without great care. If you dream of a drunken man, it portends that you will have a drunken mate. But if you dream of a man drinking coffee, he will be a hard worker.

TO KEEP A WIFE OR HUSBAND
CHEROKEE SHAMAN'S CHARM

To attract and fix the affections of a mate, on your wedding night, when your new spouse is sleeping, take your saliva and rub it on your spouse's breast, reciting four times:

> Your spittle, I take it, I eat it.

Repeat this ceremony for three more nights, reciting four times on the second night:

> Your body, I take it, I eat it.

And four times on the third night:

> Your flesh, I take it, I eat it.

And four times on the final night:

> Your heart, I take it, I eat it.

Then recite:

> Listen! O, now you have drawn near to
> harken, O, Ancient One. This woman's [or
> man's] soul has come to rest at the edge of your
> body. You are never to let go your hold upon it.
> It is ordained that you shall do just as you are

requested to do. Let her never think upon any other place. Her soul has faded within her. She is bound by the black threads.

This ceremony is so effective that no husband need have any fears for his wife after performing it.

AGAINST ONE'S HUSBAND LOVING ANOTHER WOMAN
TUSCAN WITCH'S CHARM

To do an evil so that a man may be drawn from loving another woman and only be attached to his wife, take three Indian chestnuts or wild-horse chestnuts and powder them as finely as possible. Then take a new earthenware pot and put into it the powder, and mix with it three drops of the husband's blood, or of the woman whom he loves, and put this blood with the rest, and, if it be possible, add to this as much more blood of either as can be obtained, and to this a half liter of spirits and some water, and boil it in a double boiler, that is, the pot in another pot of water, and when it shall have boiled for a quarter of an hour, put the pot under the bed. Then at midnight, the wife should leave the bed and bathe the head of the husband a little, in the form of a cross, and say:

> I bathe not thee, I bathe thy heart,
> That thy love from me may ne'er depart!
> That thou shall to me be true for aye!
> Nor with other women go thy way,
> Nor deal with them, be it as it may.

And this must be done for seven nights, thrice in a night. Then throw the pot and all its contents into a running stream, saying:

> Now I cast this pot away,
> With my husband's thought to stray,
> To others' love that I may see
> Him true, as I shall ever be!

And having thrown it into the water, walk away without looking behind you, and for three days after do not pass by that place.

TO CAUSE THE RETURN OF A TRUANT WOMAN
ANCIENT HINDU INCANTATION

To cause the return of a truant woman, recite:

> The heavens have stood, the earth has stood,
> all creatures have stood. The mountains have
> stood upon their foundation, the horses in the
> stable I have caused to stand.

He who has control of departure, who has control of coming home, return, and turning in, that shepherd do I also call.

O Gâtavedas, Agni, cause thou to turn ill; a hundred way's hither shall be thine, a thousand modes of return shall be thine. With these do thou restore us again!

TO ALAY JEALOUSY
ANCIENT HINDU INCANTATION

To allay jealousy in a woman or man, recite:

The first impulse of jealousy, moreover the one that comes after the first, the fire, the heart-burning, that do we waft away from thee.

As the earth is dead in spirit, in spirit more dead than the dead, and as the spirit of him that has died, thus shall the spirit of the jealous be dead!

Yon fluttering little spirit that has been fixed into thy heart, from it the jealousy do I remove, as air from a water-skin.

TO CONCEIVE A CHILD
GYPSY SPELL

To conceive a child, have a fertile woman drink the water in which the husband has spit, saying:

> Where I am flame, be thou the coals. Where I am rain, be thou the water!

TO KNOW IF A WOMAN SHALL HAVE A GIRL OR BOY
AMERICAN MAGICIAN'S CHARM

To know if a woman with child shall have a girl or boy, write the proper names of the father and mother, and the month she conceived the child; count the letters in these words, and divide the amount by seven. If the remainder be even, it will be a girl; if odd, it will be a boy.

WEATHER

AND EARTH

TO MAKE IT SNOW
AMERICAN WITCH'S SPELL

To make it snow, hold a magic object or one of great significance to you under a piece of white cloth and recite:

> Goddess Hecate, lead away the heat
> Bring only virgin snow to the ground at my feet
> Let it snow all day and night
> The animals will not stir; I will not fright
> I need snow, need it right away
> To be covered in white
> Just for one day.

TO MAKE THE WIND BLOW
AMERICAN MAGICIAN'S SPELL

To call on the four winds from the four corners of the Earth, go to the highest point possible and yell:

Eurus, Notus, Zephyrus, Boreas!

TO MAKE IT RAIN
SIA INDIAN CHANT

The following is the song of the rain:

White floating clouds,
Clouds like the plains
Come and water the earth.
Sun embrace the earth
That she may be fruitful.
Moon, lion of the north,
Bear of the west,
Badger of the south,
Wolf of the east,
Eagle of the heavens,
Shrew of the earth,
Elder war hero,
Warriors of the six mountains of the world,
Intercede with the cloud people for us,
That they may water the earth.
Medicine bowl, cloud bowl, and water vase

Give us your hearts,
That the earth may be watered.
I make the ancient road of meal,
That my song may pass over it—
The ancient road.
White shell bead woman
Who lives where the sun goes down,
Mother Whirlwind,
Father Sus'sistinnako,
Mother Ya'ya, creator of good thoughts.
Yellow woman of the north,
Blue woman of the west,
Red woman of the south,
White woman of the east,
Slightly yellow woman of the zenith,
And dark woman of the nadir,
I ask your intercession with the cloud people.

TO MAKE IT STOP RAINING
HOODOO CHARM

If you want to make it stop raining, plant a cross in the middle of the yard and sprinkle it with salt.

TO LEAD A STORM AWAY
ESKIMO SHAMAN'S SPELL

To lead a storm away, say to it:

> In what manner can I turn to the outer side
> of this big outer world; to the direction of the
> southern wind; to the direction of Ca'xcu, who
> has a black spot upon the forehead?

 ## FOR AVERTING LIGHTNING
GYPSY CHARM

Lightning can be averted by sticking a knife in a loaf of bread and spinning the two on the floor of the house while the storm lasts.

TO FIND TREASURE IN THE EARTH
GYPSY CHARM

To find treasure in the earth, a magnet made beyond perfection, accompanied by the prime material of which all metals grow, is required.

Take a compass that is beyond perfection, made from prime material. Around the compass, engrave signs representing the various treasures or ores you wish to find beneath the earth. If it is desired now to ascertain what kind of a metal is most likely to be found nearby, consult said compass and place your foot perpendicular to where it shows its attractions, and that is the direction in which treasure may be found.

TO FIND SILVER AND GOLD
GYPSY INCANTATION

To find silver and gold, proceed in the forenoon before twelve o'clock to a hazelnut shrub that was less than a year old and has two twigs. Then place yourself toward the rising sun, take the twigs in both hands, and speak:

I conjure thee, one summer long, hazel rod, by
the power of God, by the obedience of Jesus
Christ of Nazareth, God and Mary's own son,
who died on the cross, and by the power of
God, by the truth of God arose from the dead;
God the Father, Son, and Holy Ghost, who
art the very truth thyself, that thou showest me
where silver and gold is hidden.

FOR EXTINGUISHING FIRE WITHOUT WATER
GYPSY RITUAL

Inscribe the following letters upon each side of a plate
and throw it into the fire, and forthwith the fire will be
extinguished:

SATOR
AREPO
TENET
OPERA
ROTAS

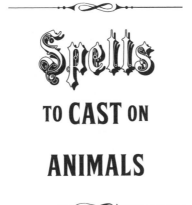

Spells

TO CAST ON

ANIMALS

TO KEEP PIGEONS SAFE AND KEEP THEM FROM ESCAPING
GYPSY SPELL

To prevent pigeons from deserting the pigeon coops or dove cots (also, that no pigeon hawk can catch them), let the pigeons be put into the cot on a Friday, and pluck off two feathers from the right wing of every pigeon before they are left to fly into the coop. Fasten these feathers by a tack in the coop, and place some stonewort or chickweed into the pigeons' drinking water. As long as the feathers remain in the coop, no pigeon will desert, and no hawk will catch them.

TO FIND A LOST ANIMAL
AMERICAN WITCH'S INCANTATION

At dusk, go to a crossroads and face the setting sun. Bow at the waist nine times while calling to the animal. Then bow at the waist nine times while reciting:

> God above, as you called forth the fish in the sea, birds in the air, and fauna on land, bring forth your brother [or sister] [Name of animal].

Then bow nine final times while calling the animal once more. Before leaving the crossroads, take ten steps backward, without looking behind you. Then immediately turn around and go directly to your home before sunset.

TO KEEP WILD BEASTS AWAY
ANCIENT MACEDONIAN POTION

For not just curing the bite of serpents and other wild beasts, but also keeping them away so that the dogs flee from thee and no animal may touch thee, pound sorrel and smear the juice on thyself, and thou shall marvel.

AGAINST FURIOUS BEASTS
AMERICAN MAGICIAN'S SPELL

Repeat reverently, and with sincere faith, the following words, and you shall be protected in the hour of danger from furious beasts:

> At destruction and famine thou shall laugh, neither halt thou be afraid of the beasts of the Earth.

> For thou shall be in league with the stones of field; the beasts of the field shall be at peace with thee.

TO BECKON SNAKES FOR ANSWERS
AMERICAN WITCH'S RITUAL

To call upon the wisdom of snakes, place sprigs of lavender in a circle at nighttime, and draw the image of a snake inside. Issue a call to the spirit of snakes. Explain what you need to know and why you have called them forth. Go to straight to bed to receive an answer in your dreams.

TO HALT A SNAKE
ANCIENT MACEDONIAN SPELL

To stop a serpent coming towards thee: When thou seest it coming, say these words:

> Moses set a javelin, deliverer from harmful things, upon a column and a rod, in the form of a cross, and upon it he tied an earth-crawling serpent, and thereby triumphed over the evil. Wherefore we shall sing to Christ our God; for he has been glorified.

TO CATCH LARGE FISH
CHEROKEE SHAMAN'S CHARM

To have an abundant and large catch, the fisherman must chew a small piece of Venus flytrap and spit it upon the bait and also upon the hook. Then, standing facing the stream, place the bait upon the hook while reciting:

> Listen! Now you settlements have drawn near to hearken. Where you have gathered in the foam you are moving about as one. You Blue Cat and the others, I have come to offer you freely the white food. Let the paths from every direction recognize each other. Our spittle shall be in agreement. Let them be together as we go about. The fish have become a prey and there shall be no loneliness. Your spittle has become agreeable. I am called Swimmer. Yû!

He will be able to pull out a fish at once, or if the fish are not about at the moment, they will come in a very short time.

TO CATCH OYSTERS
AMERICAN MAGICIAN'S CHANT

During oyster dredging, charm the oysters into your net by chanting thusly:

> The herring loves the merry moonlight, the
> mackerel loves the wind; but the oyster loves
> the dredger's song, for he comes of gentle kind.

FOR ATTACHING A DOG TO A PERSON
POW-WOW POTION

Provided nothing else was used before to effect it, to make a dog attached to you, draw some of your blood, and let the dog eat it along with his food, and he will stay with you. Or scrape the four corners of your table while you are eating, and continue to eat with the same knife after having scraped the corners of the table. Let the dog eat those scrapings, and he will stay with you.

TO ATTRACT BEARS
CHEROKEE SHAMAN'S CHANT

Before the Ani-Tsâ'kahï lost their human shapes and were transformed into bears, they taught this spell to the Cherokee shaman. It is to be sung in order to attract bears to a camp for any purpose.

> *Heeeee! Hayuya'haniwä, hayuya'haniwä, hayuya'haniwä, hayuya'haniwä.*

> In Rabbit Place you were conceived; in Rabbit Place you were conceived. *Yoho-ooo!*

> *Heeeee! Hayuya'haniwä, hayuya'haniwä, hayuya'haniwä, hayuya'haniwä.*

> In Mulberry Place you were conceived; in Mulberry Place you were conceived. *Yoho-ooo!*

> *Heeeee! Hayuya'haniwä, hayuya'haniwä, hayuya'haniwä, hayuya'haniwä.*

> In *Uyâ'yë* you were conceived, in *Uyâ'yë* you were conceived. *Yoho-ooo!*

> *Heeeee! Hayuya'haniwä, hayuya'haniwä, hayuya'haniwä, hayuya'haniwä.*

> In the Great Swamp, you were conceived; in the Great Swamp, you were conceived. *Yoho-ooo!*

> And now surely we and the good bears, the best of all, shall see each other.

TO COMPEL AN ANIMAL TO FOLLOW YOU
GYPSY SPELL

To compel a dog, horse, or other animal to follow you, utter these words three time into his right ear:

> Casper guide thee, Balthazar bind thee,
> Melchior keep thee.

TO COMMUNICATE WITH ANIMALS WITH YOUR MIND
AMERICAN WITCH'S SPELL

To commune with an animal with whom you have a relationship, look into his or her eyes while envisioning a circle of light encircling you both. Close your eyes and match the rhythm of your breathing to the animal's, then think:

> I pronounce to thee my intentions, with heart and spirit high.
>
> I am here to hear, or to be.
>
> Be my animal guide.

Be aware of any message the animal may be sending.

TO UNDERSTAND THE LANGUAGE OF BIRDS
AMERICAN MAGICIAN'S CHARM

Take the tongue of a vulture and lay it for three days and three nights in honey, afterward under your tongue. Thusly, you will understand all the songs of birds.

TO MAKE CATTLE WELL
GYPSY SPELL

If cattle are ill and you do not know the nature of the disease, take two birds—quails, if possible. Kill one, but allow the other, besprinkled with the first's blood, to fly away. With what remains of the blood, sprinkle some fodder and place it before the animal, saying the words:

> What in thee is evil
> Come forth
> Here is no home
> For the evil one!
> When drops of blood come not,
> Sickness comes not,
> Thou evil one, come forth!
>
> Three white, three black,
> Three fat lie together here.
> Whoever disturbs them
> Remain to me!

TO CAUSE A COW TO GIVE A GOOD SUPPLY OF MILK
GYPSY POTION

During Christmas night, take the milt of a herring and the sinew thereof; also, bay leaves, saffron, and black caraway seed. Mix all of them together, spread upon four pieces of bread, and give it to the cow.

TO VANQUISH VERMIN
ANCIENT HINDU INCANTATION

To vanquish vermin, recite:

> Slay ye the tarda, the samanka, and the mole,
> O Asvins; cut off their heads, and crush their
> ribs! Shut their mouths, that they shall not eat
> the barley; free ye, moreover, the grain from
> danger!

Ho tarda, ho locust, ho snapper, upakvasa! As
a Brahman eats not an uncompleted sacrifice,
do ye, not eating this barley, without injury,
get out!

O husband of the tarda, O husband of the
vagha, ye of the sharp teeth, listen to me!
The rodents of the forest, and whatever other
rodents there are, all these we do crush.

FOR PROTECTION AGAINST WOLVES AND DOGS
GYPSY SPELL

So that no wolf or dog may bite or bark at you, speak the
following:

Thus did it happen, on a Friday it was, when
our Lord God rode over a field of grass, he carried neither money nor purse with him; for he
owned naught but his five holy wounds.

May God protect us against wolves, dogs, and
hounds! Saint Peter, close the locks that close
the jaws of these fearsome creatures, friend
or foe.

TO CHARM A HORSE
GYPSY INCANTATION

Horses, especially black ones, can see beings which are invisible to human eyes. To charm a horse so that he's no longer frightened of these creatures, draw with a coal a ring on his left hoof, and on his right hoof a cross, and murmur:

Round, round, and round
Be thou, be thou very sound
The devil shall not come to thee.

God, God shall be with thee
Sweet God drive away
From the horse's body
The Father of Evil!
Go not to any other man
To whom I give unto him.

Be beautiful!
Frolicsome and good,
Seven spirits of earth hear
I have seven chains,
Protect this animal
Ever, ever!

Then give a piece of salted bread to the horse, and spit seven times into his eyes. He will lose all fear for supernatural beings and no longer spook.

FOR A LIVELY HORSE
GYPSY SPELL

To have a horse that is always in good spirits and lively,
during the waning moon rub his spine with garlic, and
utter these words:

> Evil in thee,
> May the devil eat it much!
>
> Good in thee,
> May it remain in thee!

POWER

TO DREAM OF THE FUTURE
AMERICAN MAGICIAN'S SPELL

To know the future, let an egg go rotten, then place it next to your bed as you sleep. Your dreams will tell you what you need to know.

TO FIND SOMETHING LOST
CHEROKEE SHAMAN'S RITUAL

To find something lost, gather a small, well-worn pebble, as round as possible, from a lake or a stream. Tie a string around it and hold this string between your thumb and forefinger. Repeat:

> Listen! Ha! Now you have drawn near to
> hearken, O Brown Rock; you never lie about
> anything. Ha! Now I am about to seek it out.
> I have lost [Name of lost article], and now
> tell me about where I shall find it. For is it not
> mine? My name is [Name].

The pebble will swing farther toward one direction than the other. After marking your current position, go a considerable distance in the direction of the pebble, and make a second trial by repeating the formula and watching where the stone swings. Follow the direction indicated for some time, then complete a third trial. On the third trial, the stone may veer around toward the starting point, or a fourth or fifth attempt may complete the circuit.

Having thus arrived where you began, you may make the conclusion that the missing article is somewhere within this circumscribed area. Advance to the center of this space and mark out upon the ground a small circle, enclosing a cross with arms pointing toward the four cardinal points. This is the final trial. Holding the stone over the center of the cross, again repeat the formula and note the direction in which the pebble swings. Go slowly and carefully over the whole surface in that direction, between the center of the circle and the limit of the circumscribed area, until the article is found.

TO OPEN LOCKS
ANCIENT JEWISH CHARM

To open a lock, obtain the fat
from a snake and the right
foot of a raven. Rub
the fat onto the raven's
foot, then place the foot
against any lock to un-
lock the same without a key.

TO SPELL-BIND SOMETHING
POW-WOW SPELL

To fasten or spell-bind anything, say:

> Christ's cross and Christ's crown, Christ Jesus'
> colored blood, be thou every hour good. God,
> the Father, is before me; God, the Son, is beside
> me; God, the Holy Ghost, is behind me. Who-
> ever now is stronger than these three persons
> may come, by day or night, to attack me.

TO SEE IN THE DARKEST NIGHT
GYPSY CHARM

Grease your eyes with the blood of a bat and you will see
in the darkest night.

TO SEE WHAT OTHERS CANNOT SEE
GYPSY CHARM

Take a cat's eye, lay it in salt water, let it remain there for three days, then for six days in the rays of the sun. After this have it set in silver and hang it around your neck. You will see what others cannot.

THAT OTHERS CANNOT SEE YOU
GYPSY CHARM

Pierce the right eye of a bat and carry it with you, and you will be invisible. Or, obtain the ear of a black cat, boil it in the milk of a black cow, then make a thumb cover of it and wear it on the thumb.

HOW TO DISCERN SECRETS AND INVISIBLE THINGS
GYPSY POTION

If you find a white adder under a hazelnut shrub that has twelve other vipers as its twelve guardsmen with it; and the hazelnut bush under which they lay commonly bears medlars; you must eat the white adder with your other food, and you will be enabled to see and discern all secret and otherwise hidden things.

TO MAKE ONESELF INVISIBLE
EUROPEAN MAGICIAN'S RITUAL

Begin this operation on a Wednesday before the sun rises. Start with seven black beans. Take next the head of a dead man; place one of the beans in his mouth, two in his eyes, and two in his ears. Draw a figure of personal or magical significance upon his forehead. Inter the head with the face toward heaven, and every day before sunrise, for the space of nine days, water it with excellent brandy. On the eighth day you will find the cited spirit, who will say unto you: What doest thou? You shall reply:

I am watering my plant.

He will then say: Give me that bottle; I will water it myself. You will answer by refusing, and he will again ask you, but you will persist in declining, until he stretches forth his hand and shows you, suspended from the tips of

his fingers, the same figure that you traced upon the head. In this case, you may be assured that it is really the spirit of the head, because another might take you unawares, which would bring you evil, and further, your operation would be unfruitful. When you have given him your vial, he will water the head and depart. On the morrow, which is the ninth day, you shall return and will find your beans ripe. Take them, place one in your mouth, and then look at yourself in a glass. If you cannot see yourself, it is good. Do the same with the rest, or they may be tested in the mouth of a child. All those who do not answer must be interred with the head.

TO MAKE OBJECTS LEVITATE
AMERICAN MAGICIAN'S CHARM

The skill of telekinesis must be practiced and learned. To start, have a clear heart and mind. (Meditate, if possible.) Test your powers with a thin sheet of aluminum made in the shape of a cross. Balance it over the point of a tack placed on a flat surface.

While saying a prayer to Shakuni, focus your energy in a sphere around the point of the tack. Slowly turn the sphere until the cross begins moving with it. Continued in this way, your energy may begin to lift the cross from the pin.

With further meditation and practice, this skill may be transferred to other objects whose spirits have not been tarnished.

FOR FLYING
AMERICAN WITCH'S SPELL

Go to the highest point possible and repeat three times:

> Kinnaris, I sing to you,
> Take flight
> Do not leave me behind
> Give me wings
> Kinnaris ah-eh, Kinnaris.

Wait with arms outstretched for a miraculous wind to pull you up.

FOR MAKING A TRUTH SERUM
AMERICAN WITCH'S POTION

In order to induce a person to tell the truth in any manner, take the dirt from the insides of his shoes and grind it with passionflower. Place in a bottle of whisky, adding more dirt and passionflower every three days for twenty-one days. One drop on the tongue will cause the tongue to be unable to tell a lie for several minutes. Let the whisky serum age longer to lengthen the effects.

FOR MAKING A WOMAN DISCLOSE HER SECRETS
EUROPEAN WITCH'S POTION

To make a woman disclose her secrets, take the heart of a pigeon and the head of a frog. Dry them in an earthenware pot that has never been used, then grind them into a fine powder. Put the powder into a little purse, and add moss for fragrance. Put the purse under the woman's ear while she is sleeping. Fifteen minutes later she will unveil all of her secrets. Make certain to remove the purse a few minutes after she has stopped speaking; otherwise she could fall into delirium.

TO READ MINDS
AMERICAN WITCH'S RITUAL

To understand what a man is thinking without being told, you must open your mind's eye. To do so, lay down and place an amethyst in the middle of your forehead. Think about this area, your third eye, while breathing through your nose, holding your breath before each exhale. Open your mouth slightly and place your tongue between your teeth. Make your tongue vibrate by making a "th" sound each time you exhale. Repeat this twenty times for twenty nights and your mind's eye shall open.

TO BRING ABOUT SUBMISSION TO ONE'S WILL
ANCIENT HINDU INCANTATION

To bring about submission to one's will, recite:

> Your minds, your purposes, your plans, do we cause to bend. Ye persons yonder, that are devoted to other purposes, we cause you to comply!

> With my mind do I seize your minds: Do ye with your thoughts follow my thought! I place your hearts in my control: Come ye, directing your way after my course!

> I have called upon heaven and earth, I have called upon the goddess Sarasvatî, I have called upon both Indra and Agni: May we succeed in this. O Sarasvatî!

THAT ONE SHALL NOT BE DENIED ANYTHING
AMERICAN MAGICIAN'S CHARM

Take a rooster, three years old, throw it into a new earthenware pot, and pierce it through. Then put it into an ant's hill, and let it remain until the ninth day thereafter. Then take it out again and you will find in its head a white stone. Carry it on your person, and nobody will deny you anything.

TO BE TRANSFORMED INTO AN ANIMAL
AMERICAN WITCH'S SPELL

To be transformed into an animal, either wild or domestic, you must first eat and think like the animal to increase the potency of the spell. Place hair (or feathers or scales) from the animal you want to be transformed into on a flat stone. With a blessed or magic knife, slice the hair into as many pieces as possible, reciting:

> No more human strife
> I reject this body to be a [Name of animal]
> With this spell and knife
> So mote it be.

Heat the hair with sage leaves in water to make a tea, then drink it before it cools. Go to sleep where the animal sleeps.

FOR ANY WISH TO BE GRANTED
TUSCAN WITCH'S CHARM

Take a goblet or cup full of hot water and three chairs in which three girls or women of the same age must sit. Each must take a pinch of salt and put it into the boiling water all together at once. The one whose salt dissolves first will be the most fortunate. Then each must take a little bag of red woolen stuff full of ashes that have been very finely sifted; let them sit with the cup in the middle, all three clad in black with black veils, and each with a sacred wafer taken from communion. Each shall throw her ashes with the wafer into the boiling water and say:

> I do not throw the ashes,
> But I throw the wafer.
> I do not throw the wafer,
> But I throw the body and soul of [Name]
> That he may no more have peace or happiness
> Until I have obtained this my desire!

Then they must place their hands behind them, and not turn round to see the cup for a quarter of an hour; and when they at last look they will see whether the wafers are floating on the surface. In this case they will all three have obtained their wish, and if only one swims, then the one whose it is will be favored; but if none float, no favor will be granted.

FOR DELAYING DEATH
AMERICAN WITCH'S CHARM

Feathers or a bird in the room of a sick person will delay death. Resort to this only when necessary, such as when needing to delay the last breath till an absent friend arrives.

FOR ETERNAL LIFE
ANCIENT ASIATIC CHARM

Inscribe upon a piece of parchment:

Shen-Hsien.

Next, find a silverfish with magical properties that cause it to change into several different hues when eating the parchment. When a creature with these properties is found (which many take several months), eat it whole and you will be protected from death forever.

COMMUNING

WITH THE

Dead

FOR NECROMANCY
NECROMANCER'S RITUAL

Those who are desirous to raise up any Souls of the dead ought to do it in the places wherein these Souls were most known to be conversant, had some kind of affection for in times past, or impressed upon them in their life. And since the Souls of the dead are not easily raised up, except the Souls of those we know to be evil, or to have perished by a violent death, or whose bodies want a right and due burial, the places oft befitting these souls are churchyards and those places wherein there was the execution of criminal judgments or public slaughters of men.

Allure the said Souls by those things that move the very harmony of the Soul, as well as the imaginative, rational, and intellectual; such as Voices, Songs, Sound, Enchantments, and Religious Rites, which may very commodiously be administered hereunto. In raising up these Souls, perfume them with new Blood, and with Meat, Eggs, Milk, Honey, Oil, and such-like things, which give the Souls a means to receive their Bodies.

TO SPEAK TO THE DEAD WITH GHOST WATER
HOODOO CHARM

To speak to the dead, go to a graveyard at night. Place a jar of water that came from the earth on the grave of the spirit you want to commune with. If you are seeking peace, place the water on a person of peace. If you need protection, place the water on a solider. At dawn, replace the water with three pennies and an offering of rum. Use the ghost water in your ceremonies.

TO MAKE A SPIRIT-CIRCLE FOR SÉANCES
EUROPEAN MAGICIAN'S RITUAL

The spirit-circle is the assembling together of a given number of persons for the purpose of seeking communion with the spirits who have passed away from Earth into the higher world of souls. The chief advantage of such an assembly is the mutual impartation and reception of the combined magnetisms of the assemblage. These in combination form a force stronger than that of an isolated subject; first, enabling the spirits to commune with greater power; next, developing the latent gifts of mediumship in such members of the circle as are thus endowed; and finally, promoting that harmonious and social spirit of fraternal intercourse, which is one of the especial aims of the spirits' mission.

The first conditions to be observed relate to the persons who compose the circle. These persons should be, as far as possible, of contrasting physical temperaments, of opposite temperaments from one another, and as positive and negative in disposition, whether male or female. They should also be of moral character, pure mind, and not marked by repulsive points of either physical or mental condition. The number of the circle should never be less than three nor more than twelve. No person of a very strongly positive temperament or disposition should be present, as any magnetic spheres emanating from the circle will overpower that of the spirits, who must always be positive to the circle in order to produce phenomena. It is not desirable to have more than two already well-developed mediums in a circle, as mediums always absorb the magnetism of the rest of the party; hence, when there are too many present, the force, being divided, cannot operate successfully with any.

Never let the room be overheated, or even close. As an unusual amount of magnetism is liberated at a circle, the room is always warmer than it is ordinarily, and should be well ventilated. Avoid strong light, which, by producing excessive motion in the atmosphere, disturbs the manifestations. A very subdued light is the most favorable for any manifestations of a magnetic character, especially for spiritual magnetism.

If the circle is one that meets periodically, and is composed of the same persons, let them occupy the same seats (unless changed under spiritual direction) and sit around a table, their hands laid on it, with palms downward. It is believed that wood, when charged, becomes a conductor, without the necessity of touching or holding hands. If flowers and fruit are in the room, see that they are just freshly gathered, otherwise remove them; also avoid sitting in a room with many minerals, metals, or glasses, as these all injuriously affect sensitives, of whom mediums are the type.

Open the séance with prayer or music (vocal or instrumental), after which subdued, quiet, and harmonizing conversation is better than wearisome silence; but let the conversation be always directed toward the purpose of the gathering, and never sink into discussion or rise to emphasis; let it be gentle, quiet, and spiritual, until phenomena begin to be manifest. Always have a slate and chalk, or pencil and paper, on the table, so as not to be obliged to rise to procure them. Especially avoid all entering or leaving the room, moving about, irrelevant conversation, or disturbances within or without the circle-room after the séance has been once commenced. Do not admit unpunctual latecomers; nor, if possible, suffer the air of the room to be disturbed in any way after the sitting commences.

Let the séance always extend to one hour, even if no results are obtained; it sometimes requires all that time for spirits to form their battery of the materials furnished. Let it be also remembered that all circles are experimental; hence no one should be discouraged if phenomena are not produced after the first few sittings. Stay with the same circle for six sittings; if no phenomena are then produced (provided all the above conditions are observed) you may be sure you are not rightly assimilated to each other; you do not form the requisite combinations, or neutralize each other. In that case, break up, and let that circle of members meet with other persons; that is, change one, two, or three persons of your circle for others, and so on until you succeed. A humble, candid, inquiring spirit, unprejudiced and receptive of truth, is the only frame of mind in which to sit for phenomena, the delicate magnetism of which is shaped, tempered, and made or marred as much by mental as physical conditions.

When once any of the circle can communicate freely and conclusively with the spirits, the spirits can and will take charge of and regulate the future movements of the circle. Impressions are the voices of spirits speaking to our spirits, or else the admonitions of the spirit within us, and should always be respected and followed out. At the opening of the circle, one or more of the members are often impressed to change seats with others; the desire to withdraw or a strong feeling of repulsion to some member of the circle makes it painful to remain there. Let any or all of these impressions be faithfully regarded, and, at commencing, pledge to each other the promise that no offense shall be taken by following out impressions. If a strong impression to write, speak, sing, dance, or gesticulate possesses any mind present, follow it out faithfully. It has a meaning, even if you cannot at first realize it.

Strive in truth, but rebuke error gently; and do not always attribute falsehoods to lying spirits or deceiving mediums. Many mistakes occur in the communion

of which you cannot always be aware. If dark and evil-disposed spirits manifest to you, never drive them away, but always strive to elevate them, and treat them as you would mortals under similar circumstances.

All persons are subject to spirit influence and spirit guidance and control, but not all can so externalize this power as to use it consciously or be what is significantly called a medium. Even in the case of merely automatic speakers, writers, or apers, the ideas of the spirit are always measurably shaped by the idiosyncrasies and capacities of the medium. All spirit power is thus limited to expression by organism through which it works; conversely, remember that though spirits may control, inspire, and influence the human mind, they cannot change or re-create it. The magnetism of the spirit and the spirit-circle are but a quickening fire that inspires the brain, stimulates the faculties, and, like a hothouse process on plants, forces in abnormal prominence dormant or latent powers of mind, but creates nothing.

TO OBTAIN ANSWERS FROM THE SPIRITS
EUROPEAN MAGICIAN'S CHARM

To make a magic Carpet for interrogating the spirits, so as to obtain an answer regarding whatsoever matter one may wish to learn, obtain a carpet of white and new wool, and when the moon is at her full, in the sign of Capricorn and in the hour of the Sun, thou shall go into the country away from any habitation of man, in a place free from all impurity, and shall spread out thy Carpet so that one of its points shall be toward the east, and another toward the west, and having made a Circle without it and enclosing it, thou shall remain within, upon the point toward the east. Holding thy wand in the air for every operation, thou shall point in each direction and call toward the east upon Michael, toward the north upon Raphael, toward the west upon Gabriel, and toward the south upon Murial. After this thou shall return unto the point of the east and devoutly invoke the Great Name Agla, and take this point of the Carpet in thy left hand; turning then toward the north thou shall do the same, and so continuing to the other points of the Carpet, thou shall raise them so that they touch not the ground, and holding them up thus, and turning anew toward the east thou shall say with great veneration the following prayer:

> Agla, Agla, Agla, Agla; O God Almighty Who art the Life of the Universe and Who rulest over the four divisions of its vast form by the strength and virtue of the Four Letters of Thy Holy Name Tetragrammaton, Yod, He, Vau, He, bless in Thy Name this covering which I hold as Thou hast blessed the Mantle of Elijah in the hands of Elisha, so that being covered by Thy Wings, nothing may be able to injure me, even as it is said: He shall hide thee under His Wings and beneath His feathers shall thou trust, His truth shall be thy shield and buckler.

After this thou shall fold the Carpet up, saying these words following:

> Recabustira, cabustira, bustira, tira, ra, a!

When thou shall be desirous to make thine interroga-
tions, choose the night of full or of new moon, from midnight until daybreak. On the preceding evening, write
upon a slip of virgin parchment colored azure-blue, with
a pen made from the feather of a dove, the question to
which you seek answers. Thou shall transport thyself
unto the appointed spot if it be for the purpose of discov-
ering a treasure; if not, any place will serve provided it be
clean and pure. Burning incense nearby, thou shall take
thy Carpet and cover thy head and body therewith, and
prostrate thyself upon the ground, with thy face toward
the earth, before the incense beginneth to fume, keeping the fire of the same beneath the carpet, holding thy
wand upright, against which to rest thy chin. Thou shall
hold with thy right hand the aforesaid strip of parchment
against thy forehead, and thou shall say the following
words:

> *Vegale, hamicata, umsa, terata, yeh, dah, ma, baxasoxa,*
> *un, horah, himesere;* O God the Vast One, send
> unto me the Inspiration of Thy Light, make
> me to discover the secret thing which I ask of
> Thee, whatsoever such or such a thing may
> be, make me to search it out by the aid of Thy
> holy ministers Raziel, Tzaphniel, Matmoniel;
> Lo, Thou hast desired truth in the young, and
> in the hidden thing shall Thou make me know

wisdom. *Recabustira, cabustira, bustira, tira, ra, a!*
Karkahita, kahita, hita, ta!

And thou shall hear distinctly from the spirits the answer
which thou shall have sought.

FOR OBSTINATE SPIRITS
EUROPEAN WITCH'S RITUAL

If your hopes be frustrated and no Spirits will appear,
do not despair, but leave the Circle, and return again at
other times, doing as before. And if you shall judge that
you have erred in any thing, then that you shall amend,
by adding or diminishing, for the constancy of reiteration
doth often increase your authority and power, and strik-
eth terror into the Spirits, and humbleth them to obey.

Oftentimes also the Spirits do come, although they
are not visible (for they would cause terror to he that calls
them). This kind of licensing is not given simply, but by
a kind of dispensation with suspension, until they render
themselves obedient. To entice such Spirits, bring an instrument or object of the Spirit's affection, whether it be
an image, or a ring, or writing, or a candle or sacrifice, or
anything of the like sort. Use a perfume agreeable to the
Spirit. If known, call the Spirit by name. Write the name
in blood or otherwise on virgin parchment.

TO MAKE SPIRITS OBEDIENT
EUROPEAN MAGICIAN'S SPELL

To make the spirits of the dead obedient to thy call, use a
wand, and pronounce:

> I adjure and command thee, Human Spirit, to
> appear before me under the similitude of fire.
> By the ineffable Name Jehovah, by the inef-
> fable and incomprehensible Fiat, by the power
> that created all things and sustains all things, I
> conjure and adjure thee to come visibly before
> this circle. By the goodness of God when He
> created man in His own likeness, by the power
> of His justice, which expelled the demons,
> enchaining them in the Infernal Abyss; by His
> infinite mercy when He sent His Son to re-
> deem us; by all Divine Names and Attributes;
> by the omnipotence of our Savior Jesus Christ,
> destroying the works of hell, blessing the seed
> of the woman and empowering it to crush the
> serpent's head—do thou answer me and obey
> faithfully. By the ineffable Name Tetagramma-
> ton inscribed on this rod, answer me without
> deception or equivocation. Be thou obedi-
> ent unto me, a Christian baptized in the holy
> waters of Jordan. Answer me exactly, without
> enigma or pretense. Make known the power

that aids thee. I command thee by the most holy Name of God, and by the power of our Savior, Who shall judge both thee and me, the quick and the dead. I conjure thee. Come.

FOR EXORCISING THE DEAD
NECROMANCER'S SPELL

To exorcise the ghost or apparition of a departed person who was not familiar, repair with thy assistant to the churchyard or tomb where the deceased was buried exactly at midnight, as the ceremony can only be performed in the night between the hours of twelve and one. The grave is first to be opened, while the assistant beareth a consecrated torch. Holding a magic wand in your right hand, turn to each of the four winds and, touching the dead body three times with the magical wand, repeat as follows:

By the virtue of the Holy Resurrection and the torments of the damned, I conjure and exorcise thee, Spirit of [Name], deceased, to answer my liege demands, being obedient unto these sacred ceremonies, on pain of everlasting torment and distress. Berald, Beroald, Balbin, Gab, Gabor, Agaba. Arise, arise, I charge and command thee!

After these forms and ceremonies, the ghost or apparition will become visible, and will answer any questions put to it by the exorcist.

FOR EXORCISING ONE WHO DIED BY SUICIDE
NECROMANCER'S SPELL

If it be desired to put interrogatories to the spirit of any corpse that has hanged, drowned, or otherwise made away with itself, the conjuration must be performed while the body lies on the spot where it was first found after the suicide hath been committed, and before it is touched or removed. The exorcist binds upon the top of his wand a bundle of Saint John's wort with the head of an owl; and having repaired to the spot where the corpse lies, at twelve o'clock at night, he draws the circle and solemnly repeats these words:

> By the mysteries of the deep, by the flames of
> Banal, by the Power of the East and the silence
> of the night, by the Holy Rites of Hecate, I

conjure and exorcise thee, thou distressed spirit,
to present thyself here and reveal unto me the
cause of thy calamity: Why thou didst offer vio-
lence to thy own liege life, where thou art now
in being, and where thou wilt hereafter be.

Then, gently smiting the carcass nine times with the rod,
he adds:

I conjure thee, thou Spirit of [Name], deceased,
to answer my demands that I propound unto
thee, as thou ever hopest for the rest of the holy
ones and ease of all thy misery; by the blood of
Jesus which He shed for thy soul, I conjure and
bind thee to utter unto me what I shall ask thee.

Then, cutting down the carcass from the tree, they shall
lay its head toward the east; and in the space that the following conjuration is repeating, they shall set a chafing
dish of fire at its right hand, into which they shall pour a
little wine, some mastic, and lastly, a vialful of the sweet-
est oil. They shall have also a pair of bellows and some
unkindled charcoal to make the fire burn bright when the
carcass rises. The conjuration is this:

I conjure thee, thou Spirit of [Name], that thou
do immediately enter into thy ancient body
again and answer to my demands; by the virtue
of the Holy Resurrection, and by the posture

of the body of the Savior of the world, I charge
thee, I conjure thee, I command thee, on pain
of the torments and wandering of thrice seven
years, which I, by the force of sacred magic
rites, have power to inflict upon thee; by thy
sighs and groans I conjure thee to utter thy
voice. So help thee God and the prayers of the
Holy Church. Amen.

This ceremony being thrice repeated while the fire is
burning with mastic and gum-aromatic, the body will
begin to rise, and at last will stand upright before the exorcist, answering with a faint and hollow voice the questions propounded unto it: why it destroyed itself, where
its dwelling is, what its food and life are, how long it will
be ere it enter into rest, and by what means the magician may assist it to come to rest; also of the treasures
of this world, and where they are hidden. Moreover, it
can answer very punctually concerning the places where
ghosts reside and the proper manner of communicating
with them, teaching the nature of Astral Spirits and hell-
ish beings so far as its capacity alloweth. When all of this
the ghost hath fully answered, the magician ought to,
out of commiseration and reverence to the deceased, use
what means can possibly be used for procuring rest for
the spirit.

TO SUMMON A GOD OF THE DEAD
NECROMANCER'S INCANTATION

A God of the Dead may be summoned by a formula which follows. It must be spoken clearly aloud, and not a word changed, else the Spirit of the God may devour thee, as there is no food and no drink where they are. And it must be called in a secret place, without windows, or with windows only in one place, and that should be in the Northern wall of the place, and the only light shall be of one lamp, set on the altar, and the lamp need not be new, nor the altar, for it is a Rite of Age and of the Ancient Ones, and they care not for newness.

The altar should be of a large rock set in the earth, and a sacrifice acceptable unto the nature of the God should be made. And at the time of the Calling, the waters of Absu will roil, and Kutulu will stir, but unless it be His time, He will not Rise.

This is the Conjuration of the Dead God. Recite:

> May Nammatar open my eyes that I may see
> [Name of God].
> May Nammatar open my ears that I may hear
> [Name of God].
> May Nammatar open my nose that I may sense
> His approach.
> May Nammatar open my mouth that my
> voice will be heard to the far reaches of
> the Earth.

May Nammatar strengthen my right hand that
I shall be strong, to keep the Dead [Name
of God] under my power, under my very
power.

I conjure Thee, O Ancestor of the Gods!
I summon Thee, Creature of Darkness, by the
Works of Darkness!
I summon Thee, Creature of Hatred, by the
Words of Hatred!
I summon Thee, Creature of the Wastes, by the
Rites of the Waste!
I summon Thee, Creature of Pain, by the
Words of Pain!
I summon and call Thee forth, from Thy
Abode in Darkness!
I evoke Thee from Thy resting place in the
bowels of Earth!
I summon Thine eyes to behold the Brightness
of my Wand, which is full of the Fire of
Life!

I conjure Thee, O Ancestor of the Gods!
I summon Thee, Creature of Darkness, by the
Works of Darkness!
I summon Thee, Creature of Hatred, by the
Works of Hatred!
I summon Thee, Creature of the Wastes, by the
Rites of the Waste!

I summon Thee, Creature of Pain, by the
Words of Pain!
By the Four Square Pillars of Earth that sup-
port the Sky,
May they stand fast against They who desire to
harm me!
I evoke Thee from Thy resting place in the
bowels of Earth!
I summon Thee and Thine ears to hear the
Word that is never spoken, except by Thy
Father, the Eldest of All Who Know Age.

The Word that Binds and Commands is my
Word!
Ia! Ia! Ia! Nngi banna barra ia!
Iarrugishgarragnarab!

I conjure Thee, O Ancestor of the Gods!
I summon Thee, Creature of Darkness, by the
Works of Darkness!
I summon Thee, Creature of Hatred, by the
Works of Hatred!
I summon Thee, Creature of the Wastes, by the
Rites of the Waste!
I summon Thee, Creature of Pain, by the
Words of Pain!
I summon Thee, and call Thee forth, from Thy
Abode in Darkness!

I evoke Thee from Thy resting place in the
bowels of Earth!

MAY THE DEAD RISE!
MAY THE DEAD RISE AND SMELL THE
INCENSE!

This shall be recited only once, and if the God does not
appear, do not persist, but finish the Rite quietly, for it
means that It hath been summoned elsewhere, or is en-
gaged in some Work which it is better not to disturb.

TO GIVE A SPIRIT LICENSE TO DEPART
EUROPEAN WITCH'S CHARM

Having obtained of the Spirit that which you desire, or
when you are otherwise contented, license him to depart
with courteous words, giving command unto him that
he do no hurt. And if he will not depart, compel him
by powerful conjurations; and if need require, expel him
by Exorcisms, and by making contrary fumigations. And
when he is departed, go not out of the Circle, but stay,
making prayer, and giving thanks unto God and the good
Angels, and also praying for your defense and conserva-
tion; and then all those things being orderly performed,
you may depart.

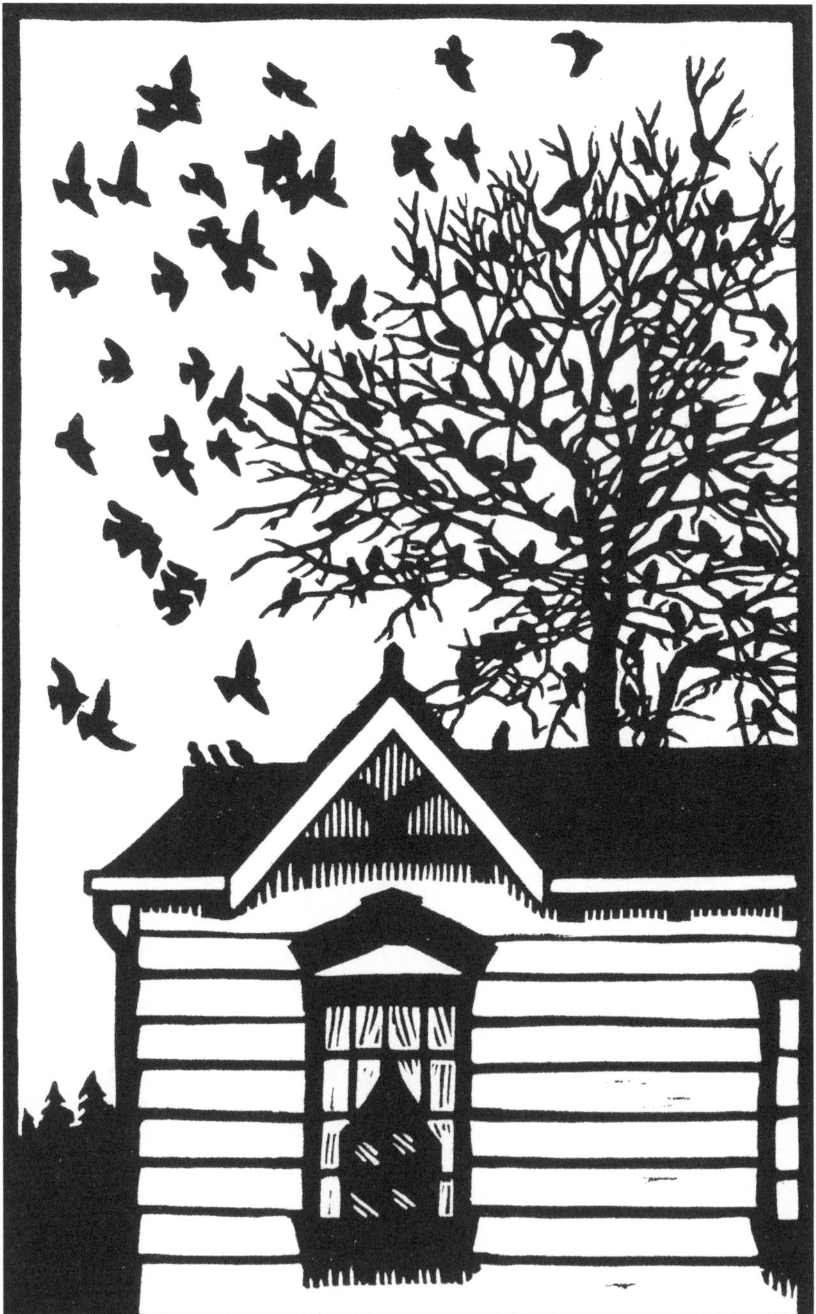

LIST OF SYMBOLS
AND OMENS

Good Omens

ANIMALS

To see an animal in an unexpected place indicates the finding of a treasure.

ARROWHEADS

To find an old flint arrow is considered lucky.

BEES

A bee flying in the house should be retained for a few minutes as a prisoner to bring luck.

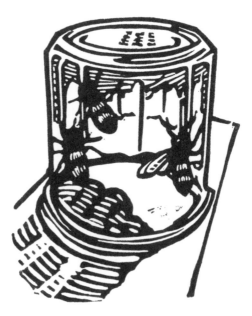

BIRDS (FLYING)

A bird on the wing is a good sign. A bird on the wing coming to you is a sign of a letter coming.

BODY PARTS, CROSSED

To sit cross-legged is considered a sign of good luck. To cross one's fingers is another way of averting evil. To cross one's fingers during a game of chance brings luck, and the reverse to your opponent.

BREAD CRUST

Carrying a crust of bread in one's pocket is considered lucky and brings prosperity.

BRIDAL BEDS

It is considered lucky for girls to sit on a bride's bed, as it will cause other marriages.

BUTTONS

To button your vest accidentally so that the buttons and holes come out uneven is a good sign.

CATS, SNEEZING

The sneezing of a cat is said to be a happy omen for a bride.

COINS

It is lucky to throw a small coin into a well of drinking water.

CORN

A red ear of corn is considered a lucky find. It should be carefully preserved until the next harvest.

CRICKETS

Crickets in the house are considered a sign of luck and prosperity, but a sign of illness if they leave without apparent reason. Do not on any account disturb a cricket in your house.

DAYS

The following days are lucky each year, especially when it comes to love.

> January 1, 2, 15, 26, 27, 28.
> February 11, 21, 25, 26.
> March 10, 24.
> April 6, 15, 16, 20, 28.
> May 3, 13, 18, 31.
> June 10, 11, 15, 22, 25.
> July 9, 14, 15, 18.
> August 6, 7, 10, 11, 19, 20, 25.
> September 4, 8, 9, 17, 18, 23.
> October 3, 7, 16, 21, 22.
> November 5, 14, 20.
> December, 14, 15, 19, 20, 22, 23, 25.

DOVES

A dove alighting on a ship is a sign of favorable winds.

DUCKS

Ducks are good, for sailors especially. They foretell safety from drowning.

EYEBROWS, JOINED

When a woman's eyebrows meet across her nose, it is a good sign. She will be happy whether she marries or not.

HORSES

Seeing a horse is lucky, especially a brown or gray horse. Spit on your little finger and rub it on a horse, and money will come to you.

HORSESHOES

Horseshoes are always considered lucky, and should be hung over the door of the house or barn. A horseshoe on your barn insures a good harvest.

KNIVES, DROPPING

If a knife be dropped accidentally so that its point penetrates the ground and it stands upright, good luck will result.

LADDERS, CLIMBING

To climb a ladder with an odd number of rungs is a good sign and leads to success.

MARTINS

Martins nesting under your eaves bring good luck if undisturbed.

MOLES

A mole on the forehead brings good fortune, so also one on the chin. Hairs growing out of moles are especially lucky; they are considered harbingers of wealth.

MOON, NEW

The new moon first seen over the right shoulder offers an opportunity for a wish to come true.

MOTHS

To kill a moth hovering about a candle is to invite good luck.

PEAS

To find nine peas in a pod is a forerunner of luck.

ROBINS

A robin is a bringer of good luck if it flies into the house.

ROOSTERS

A rooster looking toward you is an excellent sign.

SHAMROCKS

The fortunate possessor of the four-leaved shamrock will have luck in gambling and racing, and witchcraft will have no power over him. But he must always carry it about his person, and never give it away, or even show it to another.

SHOOTING STARS

If you observe a shooting star, make a wish while it is still in motion, and the wish will come true. A sick person witnessing a shooting star will recover within the month.

SNAILS, BLACK

If you see a black snail, throw it over your head for luck.

SNEEZING

To sneeze three times in rapid succession is considered a good omen. If someone sneezes after you have made a statement, it places the seal of truth upon it, and the statement may not be doubted.

SPIDERS

Long-legged spiders are harbingers of good fortune. A small red spider—called sometimes a money spinner—running over you is a sign of money coming to you. Do not in any way disturb it.

SWANS

Shouldst thou see a swan on Friday, in the joyous morning dawn, there shall be increase on thy means and thy kin, nor shall thy flocks be always dying.

TEAKETTLES, SINGING

If your teakettle sings, it is a sign of happiness and contentment in your home.

WATER JUGS

It is lucky to meet a woman carrying a jug full of water or other liquid, but unlucky if it be empty.

WINE, SPILLING

To spill wine whilst drinking a toast is a good omen and brings health and happiness to the one concerned.

Bad Omens

ANIMALS, LYING

A beast lying down is ominous. It foretells a sickness, continued illness, or death.

BATHING

Should you wash your hands or face in water just used by another, be sure to first sprinkle a few drops on your head before emptying the vessel, to avoid bad luck.

BELLOWS

It is a bad omen to find the bellows on the dining table.

BLINDS, FALLING

The fall of a window blind is accounted unlucky, but the evil can be averted by at once replacing it in its sockets.

BRAGGING

To brag about good health or success invites the envy of the powers of evil, and to counteract this you must, according to some authorities, touch wood; while according to others, you should knock on wood three times.

BREAD

To throw away a piece of bread is an indication of carelessness and brings bad luck. To break up your bread into crumbs at the table is an omen of coming poverty.

BROTHERS, MARRIED

It is unlucky for three married brothers to live in the same town.

BUCKETS

It is unlucky to come across an empty bucket when going out of a house, or a full bucket coming in.

CARDS, PLAYING

To play cards on a table without a cover is considered unlucky. To drop a card on the floor during a card game is a bad sign and means the loss of that game.

CATS, BLACK

The meowing of a black cat at midnight is a bad omen and foretells a death.

CHAIRS, FALLING

If a chair falls as a person rises, it is an unlucky omen.

CHICKENS

Fowls without a cock in their midst are not a good sign.

CHILDREN

Never pass a child through a window; it stops his growth. Stepping over a child does the same; therefore, whoever takes such a step inadvertently must step back again to break the evil spell.

CHURCH BELLS

When the church bell strikes while the parson is giving out his text, someone in the congregation will die.

COMBS, DROPPING

To drop a coarse comb foretells a visit by a man; dropping a fine-tooth comb means a visit from a woman.

CUTTLEFISH

An eight-armed cuttlefish is regarded by sailors as a bad omen.

ELDER-WOOD AND EVERGREEN

It is unlucky to use elder-wood or evergreen to make a fire.

FIREPLACES

When poker and tongs hang both on the same side of the fireplace, it betokens a breaking of friendship.

FLOWERS, PICKING

To pick flowers before they are in full bloom is said to cause a stye.

FOOD, DROPPING

If in eating you miss your mouth and the food falls, it is unlucky and denotes illness.

FURNITURE, CREAKING

Furniture creaking at night without visible cause is a sign of death or illness.

GLASS, BREAKING

To break a glass while drinking a toast is a bad omen, and may result in the early death of the person toasted.

HANDS, SHAKING

It is bad luck to shake hands with anyone across the table.

HANDS, WASHING

Two persons washing their hands in the same basin or using the same towel at the same time had better beware, for their friendship will be of short duration. However, making a cross with the thumb and first finger will prevent the evil from being carried out.

HOME, ENTERING

To enter a house with the left foot first brings bad luck to the occupants.

HORSES, WHITE

It is ill luck when with a funeral party to meet a man on a white horse. No matter how high the rank of the rider may be, the people must seize the reins and force him to turn back and join the procession at least for a few yards.

LADDERS, WALKING UNDER

To walk under a ladder when it is leaning against a wall is a sign of bad luck. To pass under a ladder that is hung horizontally does not influence your luck for good or evil.

LEAVING

Never leave a house by a different door from that by which you entered it; it is carrying away the good luck of the place.

MAIL

Letters crossing in the mail betoken evil fortune.

MARIGOLDS

March marigolds will cause drinking habits if looked at too long.

MIRRORS, BREAKING

To break a mirror is considered unlucky, and the person breaking the glass will have bad fortune for seven years. However, if a mirror is willfully and purposely broken and thrown away, it will have no effect on the person breaking the glass.

MONEY, UNSPENT

It is a sign of ill luck to find money and not spend it. It should be spent in a good cause, or given in charity.

MOON, NEW

It is unlucky to see a new moon for the first time through a glass.

MOON, SHADOWS

To see your shadow cast by the moon is distinctly un-lucky.

MOON, WANING

Marry at the time of the moon's waning and your good luck will wane also.

OVENS, EMPTY

It is unlucky to leave an oven empty. When you are not baking in it, keep a piece of wood within, or you may not have anything to bake.

OWLS

Owls are considered unlucky birds. Their voices are a bad omen and mean coming disaster. The continual hooting of owls at night is an omen of ill health. Never look into an owl's nest.

PENKNIVES, OPEN

To leave a penknife open after you are through with it is a sign of danger and is unlucky.

PICTURES, FALLING

The falling of a picture from the wall is universally regarded as a bad omen and, in the case of a portraits, frequently foretells the death of the original of the picture.

PRIESTS

To meet a priest first thing in the morning is a bad omen. This bad luck may be averted by throwing a pin at him.

RABBITS

A rabbit running across your path is a sign of impending ill luck.

RAVENS

Ravens are unequivocally unlucky. To have a raven fly into one's bedroom foretells disaster.

REFLECTIONS OF ONE'S FACE

It is considered ill luck to see your face in a mirror by candlelight.

RINGING NOISES

Ringing sounds in the ear foretell trouble.

SALT, SPILLING

To spill salt on the table is considered unlucky. To counteract the spell, throw a pinch of the salt over the left shoulder.

SHOES

It is considered unlucky to put on your left shoe first.

SILVERWARE, CROSSED

To cross knives or forks at table is a sign of bad luck.

SINGING

If you sing before breakfast you may expect bad news and sorrow before night.

STUMBLING DOWN STAIRS

To stumble in the morning on coming downstairs is a sign of ill luck during the day.

SWEEPING

It is unlucky to sweep out a room at night, and never sweep the dust from your home out of the front door. It indicates that your good luck will be swept out with it. A table should never be brushed off with a broom, as it may bring poverty.

TROUSERS

Trousers made on Friday are unlucky and will soon tear.

VOYAGES, STARTING

It is unlucky to be recalled after starting away on a voyage. At least a day should be allowed to elapse before starting out again.

Truths, Customs, and Rules

ALBATROSSES

For sailors, an albatross brings good luck and creates favorable winds. To kill an albatross is an omen of very bad luck at sea.

BATS

If a bat flies into your home, it is a harbinger of rain.

CAKES

The first cake taken out of an oven should be broken, not cut; otherwise all the rest of the cakes baked that day will be soggy.

CANDLES

A spark on the wick of a candle means a letter will be received by the one who first sees it.

CATS, BLACK

If you start out to undertake any new work or to hunt and a black cat crosses your path, you will be very lucky in your undertaking. If you try to coax a black cat to come and he runs away, you will be disappointed in your results.

CATS' PAWS

When a cat licks her paws, be prepared for company.

CLOTHING

To put your clothes on the wrong way is a sign of good luck, if performed without intention. However, the clothes must be worn that way, else the luck changes.

CUCKOOS

When you hear a cuckoo cry, take your money out of your pockets and spit on it for luck. It is a bad sign not to have any money in your pocket when you hear the cuckoo's first cry in spring.

DREAMS

Never tell your dreams before breakfast (lest they come true), and always tell them first to a woman named Mary.

EPIDEMICS

In case of an epidemic, never open the door of your home to anyone until he has knocked three times.

HAIR CUTTINGS

The cuttings of your hair should not be thrown where birds can find them; for they will take them to build their nests, and then you will have headaches all the year after.

HOMES

To move into a new home on Friday is unlucky; however, Monday and Wednesday are particularly fortunate. Never live in a house you built before it has been rented for at least a year.

HORSE TEETH

If, by accident, you find a back tooth of a horse, carry it about with you as long as you live, and you will never want money; but it must be found by chance.

ITCHING

An itching in the right palm means coming gain; in the left, coming loss. If the itch is in the elbow, you will be changing beds; if the ear itches and is red and hot, some one is speaking ill of you.

LIGHT, EXTINGUISHING

Do not put out a light while people are at supper, or there will be one less at the table before the year is out.

MISTLETOE

A girl standing under a piece of mistletoe at Christmastime may be kissed by any man who finds her there. If she refuses to be kissed, she invites bad luck. If she be kissed seven times in one day, she will marry one of the lucky seven fellows within a year.

MONEY, WON

Money that is won should be carried loose in the pocket, and not in a purse or wallet. It will then pave the way for more.

NEW YEAR'S DAY

If New Year's Day falls upon a Sunday, a quiet and gloomy winter may be expected, followed by a stormy spring, a dry summer, and a rich vintage. When New Year's Day comes on a Monday, a varied winter, a good spring, a dry summer, and an inferior vintage may be expected. When New Year's comes on a Wednesday, a hard, rough winter; a blustery, dreary spring; an agreeable summer; and a blessed vintage may be hoped for. If the first of the year happens to come on Thursday, a temperate winter, agreeable spring, dry summer, and very good vintage will follow. If on a Friday the year begins, a changeable, irregular winter; fine spring; dry and comfortable summer; and rich harvest will be the result. If New Year's Day comes on a Saturday, a rough winter with bleak winds, a wet and dreary spring, and the destruction of fruit will be the consequence.

PINS

If you see a pin, pick it up, as it will bring you good luck; to let it lie is bad luck.

PIGS

If you meet a sow coming toward you, it is an excellent omen; but should she turn from you, the luck is lost.

ROOSTERS

If a rooster stands upon the threshold of your house and crows, a stranger may be expected.

SOOT

If a leaf of soot hangs in the grate, it announces the coming of a guest.

SPARKS

A red spark on the wick of a candle signifies a letter coming to the person who sees it first.

TEAPOTS

If you neglect to close down the lid of your teapot, a guest will come and have tea with you.

The Meaning of Colors

WHITE

Also represented by the diamond or silver, white is the emblem of light, religious purity, innocence, virginity, faith, joy, and life. It indicates integrity and peace.

GREY

Grey, the color of ashes, signifies mourning, humility, and innocence accused. It can also be used in neutralizing and canceling charms.

BLACK

Black expresses the earth, darkness, wickedness, negation, and death. It can also be used when banishing evil.

RED

Red, the ruby, signifies fire, divine love, heat or the creative power, and royalty. In a bad sense red signifies blood, war, hatred, and punishment. Red and black combined are the colors of an evil, sensual mind.

BLUE

Blue, the sapphire, expresses faith, truth, constancy, devotion, and fidelity. It is used to inspire patience and understanding. It can also be the color of good health.

YELLOW (OR GOLD)

Yellow and gold are the symbols of the sun and the goodness of the soul. These colors can also signify learning, confidence, and wealth. In a bad sense, yellow signifies inconstancy, jealousy, and deceit.

GREEN

Green, the emerald, is the color of spring; of hope, particularly hope of immortality; and of victory, as the color of the palm and the laurel. It is used for rejuvenation and fertility.

VIOLET

Violet, the amethyst, signifies love and truth, or passion and suffering. It can be used to amplify other energies or increase magical power.

CONJURATIONS
BY DAY

FOR SUNDAY

Sunday's conjuration is to Surgat. His office is to discover and transport all treasures and perform anything that you may will. This experience is to be performed at night from eleven to one o'clock. He will demand a hair off your head, but give him one of a fox, and see that he takes it. Write in your circle:

> TETRAGRAMMATON, TETRAGRAMMATON, TETRAGRAMMATON. ISMAEL, ADONAY, IHUA.

And in a second circle:

> Come, SURGAT! Come, SURGAT! Come, SURGAT!

Then repeat the following conjuration:

> I conjure thee, O Surgat, by all the names which are written in this book, to present thyself here before me, promptly and without delay, being ready to obey me in all things, or, failing this, to dispatch me a Spirit with a stone that shall make me invisible to everyone whensoever I carry it! And I conjure thee to be submitted in thine own person, or in the person of him whom thou shall send me, to do and accomplish my will and all that I shall command, without harm to me or to anyone, so soon as I make known my intent.

FOR MONDAY

Monday's conjuration is to Lucifer, the Demon Lord. This experience is commonly performed in the circle between eleven o'clock and noon or three and four o'clock in the evening. Use coal or consecrated chalk to compose the circle, about which these words must be written:

> I forbid thee, LUCIFER, in the name of the
> Most Holy Trinity, to enter within this circle.

A mouse must be provided to give him; the master must have holy water and wear a stole, alb, and surplice. He must recite the Conjuration in a lively manner, commanding sharply and shortly, as a lord should address his servant, with all kinds of menaces:

> I conjure thee, Lucifer, by the living God, by
> the true God, by the holy God, Who spake and
> all was made, Who commanded and all things
> were created and made! I conjure thee by
> the Ineffable Names of God, On, Alpha, and
> Omega; Eloy, Eloym, Ya, Saday, Lux, Mugiens,
> Rex, Salus, Adonay, Emmanuel, Messias; and

I adjure, conjure, and exorcise thee by the
Names which are declared under the letters V,
C, X, as also by the Names Jehovah, Sol, Agla,
Riffasoris, Oriston, Orphitne, Phaton Ipretu,
Ogia, Speraton, Imagon, Amul, Penaton, Soter,
Tetragrammaton, Eloy, Premoton, Sitmon,
Perigaron, Irataton, Plegaton, On, Perchiram,
Tiros, Rubiphaton, Simulaton, Perpi, Klari-
mum, Tremendum, Meray, and by the most
high Ineffable names of God, Gali, Enga, El,
Habdanum, Ingodum, Obu Englabis, do thou
make haste to come, or send me [Name of person to serve as servant], having a comely and
human form, in no ways repulsive, that he may
answer in real truth whatsoever I shall ask him,
being also powerless to hurt me, or any person
whomsoever, either in body or soul.

FOR TUESDAY

Tuesday's conjuration is to Frimost, the Demon of Lust.
This experience is to be performed in its proper circle at
night from nine to ten o'clock. Give the first stone found
to Frimost. He is to be received with dignity and honor.
Compose the circle with coal or consecrated chalk, and
write about it:

> Obey me, FRIMOST! Obey me, FRIMOST!
> Obey me, FRIMOST!

Then recite this conjuration:

> I conjure and command thee, Frimost, by all
> the names wherewith thou canst be constrained
> and bound! I exorcise thee, Nambroth, by thy
> name, by the virtue of all spirits, by all char-
> acters, by the Jewish, Greek, and Chaldean
> conjurations, by thy confusion and malediction,
> and I will redouble thy Pains and torments
> from day to day forever, if thou come not now
> to accomplish my will and submit to all that I
> shall command, being Powerless to harm me,
> or those who accompany me, either in body
> or soul.

FOR WEDNESDAY

Wednesday's conjuration is to Astaroth, the Demon of
Vanity and Laziness. This experience is to be performed
in its circle at night, from ten to eleven o'clock; it is de-
signed to obtain the good graces of the King and others.
Write in your circle as follows:

> Come, ASTAROTH! Come, ASTAROTH!
> Come, ASTAROTH!

Then summon him thusly:

> I conjure thee, Astaroth, wicked spirit, by the
> words and virtues of God, by the Powerful
> God, Jesus Christ of Nazareth, unto Whom all

demons are submitted, Who was conceived of
the Virgin Mary. By the mystery of the Angel
Gabriel, I conjure thee; and again in the name
of the Father, and of the Son, and of the Holy
Ghost; in the name of the glorious Virgin Mary
and of the Most Holy Trinity, in Whose honor
do all the Archangels, Thrones, Dominations,
Powers, Patriarchs, Prophets, Apostles, and
Evangelists sing without end.

Hosannah, Hosannah. Hosannah, Lord God of
Hosts, Who art, Who was, Who art to come, as
a river of burning fire! Neglect not my commands, refuse not to come. I command thee by
Him Who shall appear with flames to judge the
living and the dead, unto Whom is all honor,
praise, and glory. Come, therefore, promptly.
Obey my will; appear and give praise to the
true God, unto the living God, yea, unto all
His works; fail not to obey me; and give honor
to the Holy Ghost, in Whose name I command
thee.

FOR THURSDAY

Thursday's conjuration is to Silcharde, a powerful
Demon who renders man happy and also discovers treasures. This experience is to be made from three to four
o'clock in the morning, at which hour he is called and
appears in the form of a King. A little bread must be

given to him when he is required to depart. Write about
your circle as follows:

Holy God! Holy God! Holy God!

Then recite:

I conjure thee, Silcharde, by the image and
likeness of Jesus Christ our Savior, Whose
death and passion redeemed the entire human
race, Who also wills that, by His Providence,
thou appear forthwith in this place. I command
thee by all the Kingdoms of God. I adjure and
constrain thee by His Holy Name, by Him
Who walked upon the asp, Who crushed the

lion and the dragon. Do thou obey me and fulfill my commands, being Powerless to do harm unto me or any person whomsoever, either in body or soul.

FOR FRIDAY

Friday's conjuration is to Bechard, the Demon of Violent Storms. This experience is to be performed at night from eleven to twelve o'clock, and a nut must be given to him.

Write within your circle:

Come, BECHARD! Come, BECHARD! Come, BECHARD!

Then recite the conjuration:

I conjure thee, Bechard, and constrain thee, in like manner, by the Most Holy Names of God, Eloy, Adonay, Eloy, Agla, Samalabactay, which are written in Hebrew, Greek, and Latin; by all the sacraments, by all the names written in this book; and by him who drove thee from the height of Heaven. I conjure and command thee by the virtue of the Most Holy Eucharist, which hath redeemed men from their sins; I conjure thee to come without any delay, to do and perform all my biddings, without any prejudice to my body or soul, without harming my book, or doing injury to those who accompany me.

FOR SATURDAY

Saturday's conjuration is to Guland, the Demon of Disease. This experience is to be performed at night from eleven to twelve o'clock, and as soon as he appears, burnt bread must be given him. Ask him anything that you will, and he will obey you on the spot. Write in his circle:

> Enter not, GULAND! Enter not, GULAND! Enter not, GULAND!

And repeat:

> I conjure thee, O Guland, in the name of Satan, in the name of Beelzebub, in the name of Astaroth, and in the name of all other spirits, to make haste and appear before me. Come, then, in the name of Satan and in the names of all other demons. Come to me, I command thee, in the Name of the Most Holy Trinity. Come without inflicting any harm upon me, without injury to my body or soul, without maltreating my books or anything that I use. I command thee to appear without delay, or, that failing, to send me forthwith another Spirit having the same Power as thou hast, who shall accomplish my commands and be submitted to my will. He whom thou shall send me, if indeed thou comest not thyself, shall in no manner depart until he hath in all things fulfilled my desires.

FOR INCREASED POWER

To give your conjuration extra power, especially if seeking treasures hidden by men or spirits, repeat the following:

> I command you, O all ye demons dwelling in
> these Parts, or in what Part of the world soever
> ye may be: by whatsoever Power may have
> been given you by God and our holy Angels
> over this place; by the Powerful Principality of
> the infernal abysses; and also by all your breth-
> ren, both general and special demons, whether
> dwelling in the East, West, South, or North, or
> in any side of the Earth; and, in like manner, by
> the power of God the Father; by the wisdom of
> God the Son; by the virtue of the Holy Ghost;
> by the authority I derive from our Saviour Jesus
> Christ, the only Son of the Almighty and the
> Creator, Who made us and all creatures from
> nothing, Who also ordains that you do hereby
> abdicate all Power to guard, habit, and abide in
> this Place. I constrain and command you, *nolens
> volens*, without guile or deception, to declare me
> your names and to leave me in peaceable pos-
> session of this Place. Of whatsoever legion you
> be, and of whatsoever part of the world; by or-
> der of the Most Holy Trinity and by the merits
> of the Most Holy and Blessed Virgin, as also of

all the saints, I unbind you all, spirits who abide in this place, and I drive you to the deepest infernal abysses. Thus: Go, all Spirits accursed, who are condemned to the flame eternal that is prepared for you and your companions, if ye be rebellious and disobedient. I conjure you by the same authority, I exhort and call you, I constrain and command you, by all the Powers of your superior demons, to come, obey, and reply positively to what I direct you, in the Name of Jesus Christ. Whence, if you or they do not obey promptly and without tarrying, I will increase your torments for a thousand years in hell. I constrain you therefore to appear here in comely human shape, by the Most High Names of God, Hain, Lon, Hilay, Sabaoth, Helim, Radisha, Ledieha, Adonay, Jehovah, Yah, Tetragrammaton, Sadai, Messias, Agios, Ischyros, Emmanuel, Agla, and Jesus Who is Alpha and Omega, the beginning and the end, that you be justly established in the fire, having no Power to reside, habit, or abide in this Place henceforth; and I require your doom by the virtue of the said Names, to wit, that Saint Michael drive you to the uttermost of the infernal abyss, in the Name of the Father, and of the Son, and of the Holy Ghost. So be it.

SOURCES

AMERICAN MAGICIANS
The Book of Forbidden Knowledge. Detroit: Johnson Smith & Co.
Young, R.F. *The Magic Wand and Medical Guide.* New York,
1875.

AMERICAN WITCHES
Gardner, Gerald. *The Gardnerian Book of Shadows.* 1949.
Peabody, Josephine Preston. *The Singing Leaves: A Book of Songs
and Spells.* Boston: Houghton, Mifflin, & Company, 1903.
("To Make Oneself Happy" and "To Gain Strength.")
Original material by Anastasia Greyleaf and the Moonbeam
Coven.

ASIATIC
Shah, Idries. *Oriental Magic.* Octagon Press Ltd., 1956.

CHEROKEE
Mooney, James. *Sacred Formulas of the Cherokees.* Bureau of
American Ethnology (7th Annual Report). Washington:
Government Printing Office, 1891.

ESKIMO
Bogoras, Waldemar. "The Eskimo of Siberia," *The Jesup North
Pacific Expedition (Volume VIII).* Leiden, Netherlands: E.J.
Brill Ltd, 1913.

EUROPEAN MAGICIANS

Agrippa, Henry Cornelius (trans. by Robert Turner). *The Fourth Book of Occult Philosophy, or Of Magical Ceremonies: The Fourth Book.* London, 1655.

The Grand Grimoire. c. 1524

Mathers, S. Liddell MacGregor, *The Key of Solomon the King.* 1888.

Waite, Arthur Edward. *The Book of Ceremonial Magic.* London, 1913.

GAELIC

Carmichael, Alexander (trans.), *Carmina Gadelica: Hymns and Incantations.* 1900.

MacKenzie, William (trans.), *Gaelic Incantations, Charms and Blessings of the Hebrides.* Northern Counties Newspaper and Printing and Publishing Company, Ltd., 1895.

Wilde, Lady Francesca Speranza. *Ancient Legends, Mystic Charms, and Superstitions of Ireland.* Boston: Ticknor and Co., Publishers, 1887.

GYPSY

The Egyptian Secrets of Albert Magnus. Allentown, 1869.

Leland, Charles Godfrey. *Gypsy Sorcery and Fortune Telling.* 1891.

Note: Spells referred to as "gypsy" may be spells by the Romany ("gypsy") people, or simply spells called "gypsy" spells by Westerners (though they may or may not have originated with the Romany).

HINDU

Bloomfield, Maurice (trans., 1897). *Hymns of the Atharva-Veda.* c. BCE 200.

Laurence, L.W. *The Great Book of Magical Art, Hindu Magic and East Indian Occultism*. Chicago: The de Laurence Company, 1915.

HOODOO
Hearn, Lafcadio. "New Orleans Superstitions," *Harper's Weekly*, 25 December, 1886.
Original material by anonymous.

JEWISH
Jubelschrift zum 70. Geburtstage des Prof. Dr. H. Graetz. 1887.
Trachtenberg, Joshua. *Jewish Magic and Superstition: A Study in Folk Religion*. Philadelphia: University of Pennsylvania Press, 2012.

MACEDONIAN
Abbot, George Frederick, *Macedonian Folklore*. Cambridge: Cambridge University Press, 1903.

NECROMANCERS
Simon (introduction), *The Necronomicon*

POW-WOW
Hoffman, John George. *Pow-Wows, or Long Lost Friend*. 1820.

SIA AND SIOUAN INDIANS
Bureau of American Ethnology (11th Annual Report). Washington: Government Printing Office, 1894.

TUSCAN WITCHES
Leland, Charles Godfrey. *Etruscan Roman Remains in Popular Tradition*. New York: Scribner's and Sons, 1892.
Scot, Reginald. *Discoverie of Witchcraft*. London, 1584

INDEX